Food Co-ops
for Small Groups

Food Co-ops
for Small Groups

by Tony Vellela

**Workman Publishing Company
New York**

Library of Congress Cataloging in Publication Data

Vellela, Tony.
    Food co-ops for small groups.

    Bibliography.
    1. Cooperative societies—United States. I. Title.
HD3284.V44   334'.5   75-9504
ISBN 0-911104-55-0 pbk.

Cover design: Paul Hanson
Jacket art: Simms Taback
Typeset: Trade Composition
Printed and bound by the George Banta Company
Manufactured in the United States of America

Workman Publishing Company
231 East 51 Street
New York, New York 10022

First printing, May 1975

To my mother, Carrie Vellela, who taught us cooperation before it was a movement or had anything to do with saving money

Everyone has a basic right to a choice of good food.

Acknowledgments I would like to thank the dozens of people who offered their assistance, information, energy and encouragement to this project—people like Natalie Silverstein and Joe James in New York City; Don Myers and Ed Smith of People's Resources in the Bronx; David Zinner in Chicago; Jeff Cox, Ray Wolf and Carol Turko at Rodale Press; Steve Hoag in East Stroudsburg; Greg Hoake in Washington, D.C.; Ed Place in Philadelphia; Sue White in Austin; Susan Youngdahl in Park Forest; Kelley in Fayetteville; Don Lubin in Allston; Steve and Patti Zimmer in Rochester; and the Workman people. Special thanks to Lori Weiner in Chicago, and Michael Schedler and Steven Hale in New York City; continuing thanks to Howard Alan Fink, for living through every stage of its production.

Contents

Part I: First Steps Toward Your Co-op

Part II: Researching Your Co-op's Needs

Food

Systems for Handling The Money

Systems for Handling The Distribution Of Food

Systems for Handling The Work

Part III: Setting Up Your Co-op

Part IV: Evaluating and Adjusting Your Co-op

Part V: Co-op Community

Appendices

Introduction

Any small group of people with the desire and the will to do so can create a food co-op that suits their needs if they have the necessary information. The purpose of this book is to provide that information in such a way that a given group can choose its own set of operating patterns and not be restricted to one model as the only method of starting a food co-op.

In 1969 the current wave of setting up food co-operatives began to ripple through a few university campuses and urban neighborhoods. Viewed then as a political as well as an economic alternative, they grew at a healthy rate until today there are thousands and thousands of members who pool their time, their energies, and their egos in their joint effort to obtain food economically.

Political similarities as the crucial unifying force were soon abandoned in most co-ops as members learned through experience that food co-ops must not complicate themselves with external issues that do not relate directly to their operation. This is not to say that ideologically congenial people should not join forces to run a food co-op; the point is that requirements concerning the members' politics serve to limit and weaken rather than extend and strengthen co-ops.

My experience with co-ops goes back to January 1970, when a small core of people—divided loosely into the categories of middle-class working people and hippie-type student young people (my group)—clumsily forged an alliance of necessity, and armed with the barest set of procedures supplied by a few traveling teenagers, created the Broadway Local Food Co-op on Manhattan's Upper West Side. The Local has grown from the original twelve people to nearly four-hundred households. In the process it has developed more and more sophisticated systems of doing its business as it reevaluated itself periodically, and has played a prominent role in the current movement to unite many of New York City's separate food co-ops into a loose federation which will support co-op warehousing.

Other recent co-ops grew out of equally diverse sets of circumstances, peoples, and needs. Over the past five years, the co-op concept has geared itself to the unique character of these times, addressing the food shortage, the economic crisis, the spiritual and moral resurgence, and the alternate life-style movement. There is, of course, a record of failures as well as successes, but the mistakes in practice and attitude have become clear enough now to learn from them.

The concept of co-operation germinated in the middle 1800's, during the early period of industrialization. Commonly considered the first true practical application of the concept is the Rochdale Village story in England; a small group of twenty-eight weavers in 1844 collected their skills and their ambitions, agreeing to share the burdens and rewards of a self-supporting economic colony.

Other examples of cooperation appeared in the late 1800's throughout England and Europe, particularly in Finland. There were immigrants coming to the United States who brought with them a cooperative philosophy in dealing with economic problems directly affecting their lives. Producers' co-operatives, particularly farm co-operatives, became fixtures in the economic life of the Midwest, and still operate today.

Co-ops on the consumer level flowered in the 1930's, backed in part by the labor union movement. Some of these small co-ops grew to the point of making it impossible for them to continue with direct member participation. Managers were hired, then a paid staff, and now they are operated like supermarkets, the only difference being that they are run on a cooperative, profit-sharing basis.

The Co-operative League of the United States, which had its origins in 1916, has collected and organized hundreds of cooperative enterprises, and is today a major source of the most valuable materials on the history, trends, pitfalls, and patterns of food cooperatives in this country from their beginnings to the present time. Books and pamphlets listed in the bibliography, available in many public and school libraries, cover extensively the history and changes of the cooperative movement.

The basic principles of all these experiences remain basic to nearly all co-ops today. They are:

—one member, one vote

—open membership

—any profits to be distributed back to members as patronage refunds

—education on co-operation for members

—membership control of the organization

Since 1969 the food co-ops that have sprouted so ambitiously in almost every city and state trace their roots to a specific need and primarily serve small groups of people. The almost spontaneous generation of these groups attests to the need that existed, and therefore to their ability to fill the demands of their members.

Why Co-ops

Any small group of people can create a food co-op, and develop a system which suits them specifically. It can be as simple or as complex as its members wish to make it, and it can change as they change.

You may find yourself looking into co-ops for the first time, prompted by a need to save money on household food bills. Or you may want to regain some measure of control over this aspect of your life. A tenants' association in your apartment building, an active role in the community planning board, a civilian review panel or the establishment of a neighborhood day-care facility or recycling center may have opened your eyes to ways you can initiate positive changes in your day-to-day activities.

You may be seeking an easier method of obtaining foods that are not readily or inexpensively available, such as dried fruits, grains, natural and organic foods or ethnic foods. You may be attracted to the sense of community that can come from participating in a food co-op.

Inexpensive food is the most often mentioned factor in creating a food co-op. Savings from 30 percent to 60 percent on average food bills are commonplace among those who use their co-ops fully. And the time it takes to complete whatever volunteer tasks need doing rarely exceeds the time spent in marketing, bargain-hunting or comparison-shopping trips to the grocer and the supermarket.

Since the greatest savings can be realized in fresh fruits and vegetables, it's common for people to take the co-op opportunity to switch from the generally more expensive, canned and processed produce, which is also less nutritious, to the thriftier fresh counterparts.

The idea of dealing with farmers and other food producers directly—not through the vast supermarket/agribusiness/Madison Avenue complex—gives some people a feeling of having a real connection with the food that eventually winds up in their bodies. A primary goal of some co-ops is to deal with producers or farmers only, and eliminate transactions with middlemen of any kind. A co-op network in Vermont and the co-op community in Austin are two examples of this philosophy.

Many others cherish the interaction with friends and neighbors a co-op affords. Since any co-op requires a certain degree of participation from its members, existing friendships are strengthened and new ones formed as the weeks and months go by. You may find youself spending an hour some evening with the folks down the block, or the latter half of an afternoon with the new people who just moved in upstairs. A food co-op brings you together for a pleasant, common purpose.

If you and a small group of friends, neighbors, relatives, or co-workers wish to create a food co-op for any of these reasons, or any other reason, then study each step in this book carefully.

Information, trust and preseverance are all equally important in creating, sustaining, and building a solid, versatile food co-op.

A "small group" can be as few as five or six people, or as

many as thirty. As you read on, you will discover how various systems apply to various sizes of groups.

At its most basic level, a co-op collects individual orders for particular food items, combines them, and purchases the total quantity at a bulk at wholesale prices. The bulk quantity is then divided among the individuals. In this case foods, purchased collectively, are cheaper because the co-op members have spent time not money. The very concept of a food co-op is explained by its name—a group co-operatively run that deals in food. The food part is easy to keep in mind; it's the co-operative part that you must strive to remember at all times!

Three general activities constitute all forms of food co-op mechanics:

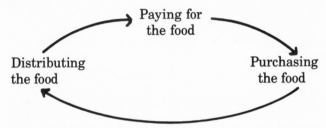

Paying for the food

Distributing the food

Purchasing the food

Once the system your group adopts is established, this circle of procedures will fall into a sequence according to the group's needs. Some systems include ordering and paying for the food in advance, then purchasing the bulk order, and then distributing it to each household. Other systems function well with members purchasing bulk amounts of food, then receiving individual orders, and finally paying. A very detailed explanation of all these systems and their variations follows on upcoming pages. For now, keep in mind that these three activities (paying, buying and distributing) form the basis of your eventual system.

Each of these three basic steps may be subdivided and organized dozens of ways. Different numbers of people may be needed to run each step, according to how you set up your co-op and how large it is.

As long as the three steps occur, don't worry about reshaping your co-op to model it after any other. The parts of each step are to be executed by the group's own members, and therefore the system you use must be tailored to them. For example, ordering your own household's food can take place before the bulk buying, or after distribution (for next week) while you're picking up this week's food, or when you pay for your food; reclaiming money for food that was not available may take place when you get your food, or at the time you order your next batch of groceries, or may be subtracted from your next bill in the form of credit; dividing up the list of volunteer tasks among members may occur when food is ordered, or when food is paid for, or when food is distributed, or at some special periodic meeting.

An order form of some sort is generally used by most co-ops as a means of recording each household's food order. This form lists the foods available, the name and address of the person doing the ordering and may also include the cost of each food item. The exact details of how order forms are drawn up, duplicated, and made available to members will come later. For now, keep in mind that the device of using a duplicated form for listing what foods you want is a very common one.

The real beauty of a co-op, especially when it's created by a small circle of people who know each other, is that it can be run the way that best suits that particular group. It's their show, their operation, serving their special needs. I personally urge new groups to nurture this flexible feature of co-ops, and never to let an ongoing procedure (tradition) or a previously learned pattern (routine) keep them from altering, widening, reorganizing, refocusing, challenging, or sprucing up their initial set of decisions about how to operate.

There are as many varieties of food co-ops as there are varieties of foods. Some co-ops handle only meats, some handle everything but meats. Some deal exclusively in organic foods, some in natural foods, some also carry carbonated soft drinks. One co-op I know of distributes from the back room of a laundromat; another calls a bicycle shop home base; others use apartment house lobbies, basements of churches or homes, the front porch of a health foods store, the main halls of student unions, the backs of trucks, the sides of warehouses, the lunchrooms of places of business, abandoned storefronts, thriving day-care centers, busy community services offices, chapel houses, community rooms of apartment complexes, idle theaters, organic bakeries, meditation centers, restaurants cafés, and somebody's fair weather backyard.

And their philosophies, their goals, their purposes? These co-op names—some direct and some whimsical—may give you a general idea: Richford Pennypinchers; Plain Old Food; the Meat Buyers' Club; Rosy Cheeks; the Common Market; Alternative Vittles; Karma Cafe; the Produce Collective; Mixed Nuts Co-op; Oriental Food Co-op; Cornucopia; Famine Foods; Vegetarian Co-op; Divine Light; Ongoing Picnic; Eco-Foods; Cheeses Co-op, and finally, Good Grits!

It's all here: each style of diet, every section of the country, all kinds of people.

Why This Book

This book tells how small groups can start and operate a food co-op regardless of where they live, what foods they eat, or whether or not they have any previous knowledge of how co-ops function. Variations are presented so that a group of any size can set up and run a co-op to meet its own needs. The emphasis is on basic information—checklists, suggestions, alternatives, considerations.

It's true that some variations and some suggestions cannot be applied to some groups or in some areas of the country. But circumstances can change. New people may join a co-op, while original members may move away. The fact that a food co-op is a dynamic, always in motion, should be kept strongly in mind.

Flow charts illustrate how things flow from one person or position to the next, and how they all interact. They present a visual explanation of how a particular kind of co-op operates. The flow chart pictures a process; words that are printed inside squares or rectangles refer to people, and words printed inside circles refer to processes or what a person does between one step and another.

A complete description, including flow charts, of six different types of co-ops can be found in the Appendix, which you may find useful for quick reference in checking out examples of particular procedures or facts. Material that merely describes other food co-ops is kept to a minimum.

Since food co-op terms or phrases vary in different parts of the country, I've included a glossary in the Appendix. Check there any time a word or phrase turns up that's new to you or that you feel may be used to describe something other than its usual meaning.

Read the entire book before you begin to implement any of it. Once you gain an overall picture, you and a few others can proceed with the challenging task of choosing from the alternatives available in creating and building your own food co-op.

Part I: First Steps Toward Your Co-op

First of all, what you need are spirited, adventuresome souls who can join you in taking on tasks needed to shape a new system for themselves. You should consider a sense of commitment as the main qualification in choosing the core of people who will help launch your co-op. It's true enough that various skills and kinds of experience will be important once the operation is under way; for now, what is needed is to share work with a few people (two or three would be perfectly adequate) willing to spend some hours for a very worthwhile purpose. Best friends, relatives, neighbors, or co-workers might be your colleagues—all you need to share is a reasonably similar taste in foods and a willingness to discover the possible systems that a co-op for your group could adopt.

These key people will help you in the early uncharted days. Not only will they share the load and take the responsibility, (they will also share the blame, if things slip up!) They will make the subsequent steps of growth and stability far easier, because several individuals will have had a thorough understanding of how the co-op works, when and how it began, and the reasons why certain decisions were made at the outset.

Start with People You Already Know

A small group of people who can work together to create and run a food co-op must have a few things in common. They should all be willing to share responsibilities; they should have a preference for some of the same foods; they should be part of a similar economic situation. For these reasons, I recommend starting your group with people you already know.

Locating the people you need is easier than it seems. They need not all be from the same group. Food co-ops have formed from friendships made in dozens of groups, in dozens of situations. Consider neighborhood groups, tenant associations, day care centers, church or other spiritual groups, office and factory workers, PTA groups, block associations, community centers, service clubs, the gang at the laundromat, the regulars at the health food restaurant, the area chapter of NOW, members of the union local—any of these groups can be sources for your food co-op's membership.

It is an unusual group in which everyone knows everyone else. Friends of friends are just as valid a source of initial members as personal friends once everyone realizes how important each member's role is in the early stages.

Other groups have started, and are thriving to this day, which began with people who had in common only a geographic location, and a desire to launch a co-op. Some existing literature on co-ops recommends putting up signs or flyers in laundromats, apartment house lobbies, in supermarkets, and on church or school bulletin boards to attract potential start-up people. My personal inclination is to avoid or limit this kind of recruiting, but this is not to say that this procedure is ineffective.

The prospective members' work schedules, outside obligations, financial levels, and also their degree of responsibility toward other people are all vital considerations, because the co-op's eventual success or failure depends on the reliability of each member.

Willingness to Share Work Trading time for money is the essence of co-operative buying. A trade-off is made between one "thing" that has worth (your time that you volunteer) in place of another "thing" that has worth (your money that you pay).

Each initial and subsequent member of a co-op must be willing to exchange volunteer labor for savings in money. To accept someone into the group who is unwilling to assume an equal share of the work is suicidal for the co-op. Don't invite friends or relatives to work on creating the co-op if you have seen evidence of their tendency to bypass work, either on the job, in the neighborhood, or in a community group they belong to in name only.

At this life-or-death stage in shaping a new organization, you owe it to yourself, to the other dedicated people involved, and to the basic integrity and concept of co-operatives, to weed out anyone who will not, from the outset, assume an equal, continuing share of the work.

Economic Range Money plays the pivotal role in two key areas in which a co-op functions. At the outset, whether or not members can afford to pay for food in advance is the single most important factor in determining the type of bookkeeping procedure the group will adopt.

No co-op can stay alive if it cannot support bulk orders of the foods it plans to purchase. So your group must be financially able to order and pay for a wholesale amount of food each time you shop.

This is not usually a problem for new groups, but it bears mentioning because the more thought that's put into creating your working plan, the less chance there is that it won't work, or will work poorly.

No Dilettantes or Favor-Doers In some circles, belonging to a food co-op is an "in" activity, a handy method of displaying one's individuality. A person who joins a food co-op for these reasons usually does not contribute time or ideas to the group in a meaningful way. However, if he performs all that is required in the work-and-responsibility areas, and is not taking the place of a genuinely needy individual, his motives should not be questioned.

Short-term members who do their volunteer jobs are no problem for an ongoing steady co-op to absorb. But anyone who does not expect to draw better, less expensive foods and perhaps a sense of community from this co-op should not be expected to bring insight and constructive criticism to the early planning sessions of a beginning co-op.

Do not cut yourself off from the very valuable sources of information and experience from people who may have belonged to and worked in a food co-op elsewhere, but who do not plan to stay in your area for very long. Encourage them to offer advice and suggestions on any topic you are investigating. But, of course, the final decisions should come from the people who will be the more permanent members of the co-op.

It is true that to run a co-op, you need a certain number of orders to combine into a bulk order equal to a wholesale quantity. It is also true that you may experience some delays in locating the total number of people required in order to begin.

It is *not* true that someone who cannot contribute volunteer time would be doing your group a favor by purchasing food from you.

Such a proposal is unwise for the group to accept for two reasons. First, the very nature of a co-op is equal sharing of *all* the work. If certain members do not pull their share of the work load, and are thought to be neglecting their responsibility, resentment can destroy the sense of solidarity among the other members who have been working in the belief that each member has been doing his share. Second, if you must overbuy amounts of some foods to realize a wholesale amount, your "favor-doers" may feel they can purchase this food at an appropriate markup price (for example, 5 percent, 10 percent, or 15 percent—whatever amount the members feel reflects the value of the work they do to make the co-op operate. My advice is to make this markup at least 15 percent or 20 percent, to discourage these people from taking the easy way out of working, and to encourage people to become working members of the co-op.

Agreeing on a Trial Period The decision to create a food co-op must have built into it a commitment to give it "time to grow." Like anything else, it will undergo a precarious early life, and there will be a good deal of floundering before it gains strength.

To set a trial length of time in days or weeks at this stage is unwise. The trial period should be based on a certain number of ordering cycles, say five or six. If you were to limit the co-op's trial period to two months, and it takes you one month to complete research and decide on a system, that leaves only four short weeks to test results. Worse still, if you take it slowly and create an every-other-week buying cycle, the group has only two cycles on which to base its decision.

Have the members agree to give the co-op a reasonable length of time to grow and to wait until after the research stage to decide on how long the trial period should be. However long, it should be based on a certain number of ordering cycles, not on a number of weeks.

To think of the co-op as a living thing gives everyone a keener sense of how it works. Your organization will eventually take on a life of its own, responding to many influences, becoming a center of activity, growing, and able to adjust to outside factors. If you instill in it a genuine will to survive and prosper, it can't fail.

Part II: Researching Your Co-op's Needs

The First Meeting

The research needed to begin a co-op especially tailored to your group should now begin. Once the interested persons have been located, the first general meeting can be convened to discuss the next steps that must be taken.

The types of foods your group wants, where they are available, how to buy them, what systems to use for actually running the co-op, and how to set up the co-op are all areas of information that must be researched, and each member of the group will share in the tasks of compiling this information.

Dispel any notion that you are personally in charge of the project. Determine who is centrally located in the area of prospective members and who among them is willing to host the meeting. Get suggestions for possible meeting dates and times. Ask a few people to help with the telephoning and poll the members. All should agree to abide by the most favorable time and to alter their schedules to be there. As many adults as possible from each household should be present. From the beginning, full cooperation and representation are vital.

Throughout this first meeting, ask and encourage people to refer to each other by first name as often as possible, so the group can get to know itself as quickly as possible.

Ask for a volunteer coordinator who will arrange the details of the next meeting in the same manner you did for this one.

At the very end of the meeting, a brief review of the discussion will be extremely valuable. This will prevent misconceptions about what was decided, and eliminate the possibility of someone proceeding with false information.

A checklist of what should be discussed at this meeting follows. Attempt to cover all the points.

1) Seat everyone in a circle, and ask all present to introduce themselves, telling also where they live, how many people are in their household, what work they do, and whom they initially talked to about coming to the meeting. (A sign-up sheet listing all this could be available at the door to fill in as each person arrives, and will also aid in setting up the next meeting. Don't skip the verbal introductions because of the sign-up sheet.)

2) Dispel the notion that you are personally "in charge."

3) Ask for a volunteer to take notes.

4) Discuss the basic requirements a co-op must meet.

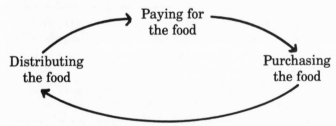

Remember that your group must develop a system in which members must collect money, choose what to buy, pay wholesalers, and then purchase and distribute the food. Outline the possible operating systems that co-ops generally use to order, pay for, and distribute their food. (At this point, some people may decide that trading time for money is not for them, and choose not to join the co-op. Expect this to happen.)

5) If there are any guests (members of other co-ops, for instance), introduce them and let them give a ten-minute description of the system their particular group uses.

6) Open the discussion to all.

7) After a while, see if there's a consensus of which operating system the group intends to use.

8) Discuss the details of the system you expect to use, and agree to give it a trial period.

9) Determine which people have particular skills they can apply to the co-op.

10) Divide up all the research that must be completed, and agree to complete it before the next meeting.

11) Set another meeting time and place to occur within the next two or three weeks.

Don't be discouraged if not all these decisions were made. People will likely want to think about the possibilities. But be certain that as much correct information as is available has been passed on to everyone present, and that as much as possible has been settled.

Membership

One strength of most co-ops is that they are flexible enough to incorporate the members' skills or particular talents into their operating systems. Recognizing what each member's skill is and remembering how fluid a new co-op can be in setting up its rules are the keys to the best utilization of all members' time and abilities. Members should be encouraged to apply experience or training they have or use in their regular occupation.

Bookkeeping skills to an outsider seem like complicated numerical entanglements that only years of schooling plus practical experience could unravel. If you were setting up a new budget for the state's educational system, or opening a new retail business, you'd be right. Your co-op, however, will create its own system for exchanging and accounting for its money, so it can be as simple or as complex as you need it to be.

Cashiers, math teachers, bookkeepers, bank tellers, business secretaries or anyone else involved in a job that requires basic familiarity with addition and subtraction of figures (not necessarily even dollars and cents) could become the bookkeeper/treasurer, or at least take the lead in developing what money system suits your group best.

Anyone who lives with or works with a mimeograph machine or an IBM, Xerox or other copier can offer a special talent that the group can use. Often, people who are employed in offices, in schools or colleges, or in any business that requires copies of its correspondence will be able to utilize this machine for a few minutes each week. New order forms and a newsletter can then be obtained with no additional charge to co-op members, and someone with a rigid daily schedule can contribute this meaningful activity as at least part of a work requirement.

Past involvement in community organizing, tenants' associations, political campaigns, student body government or any other self-run, membership-directed collection of people would yield valuable experience that can be applied directly to a food co-op. But perhaps more important are volunteer participation in accomplishing the work load, achieving consensus decisions in shaping policies, each member making allowances for individual differences among the participants, and, above all, shared trust.

Past experience in buying bulk amounts of foods would also prove valuable to draw from. Often, annual banquets, family reunions, holiday parties, or jobs in the kitchens of large institutions put one in contact with wholesalers, familiarizes one with the bulk amounts in which some foods are sold, and generally takes the scare out of buying large quantities of food at one time.

Equipment Driving to and from your sources of supply requires two important elements, one a piece of equipment and one a skill—a vehicle and someone to operate it. While in most instances the vehicle will be driven by the owner, that's not necessarily the case. My block's co-op sometimes transports the week's food in a small hatchback, but its owner is at work during the day, and his wife doesn't drive. So their contribution to the week's workload is a car and a helper. Someone else volunteers to drive. (Actually, with food for as many as thirty-five families, the job involves two or three round trips of twelve blocks each.)

Don't assume that drivers must also be lifters and loaders. Some people with bad backs can drive a 2,500-pound automobile, but cannot lift a 50-pound sack of onions.

Equipment such as an adding machine or a pocket calculator makes figuring total household orders, individual charges or per item costs of bulk amounts considerably easier and faster. You might consider borrowing one of these numerical tools until the co-op realizes enough extra money from the sale of surplus foods (or a special 1 percent tax on all foods) to purchase a good used adding machine or an inexpensive, simple-operations calculator. Neither is absolutely necessary, but either would be a handy tool indeed.

Scales to distribute bulk foods ordered by individuals by the pound can be of three types. Hanging scales, with the indicator at the top and a basket or a bin suspended from a cord to hold the items to be weighed, work well for particularly heavy items, or for loose-item foods, like lentils. Bins generally include a pour spout in their design.

Baby scales are very popular for most small orders. Simply place a container (an empty shoe box, or cardboard cheese container, or back of an egg carton) on the scale, note its weight, and add items accordingly. If the shoe box weighs 5 ounces, and you need to measure out 2 pounds of red kidney beans, pour in the beans until the scale registers 2 pounds 5 ounces. Baby scales have another benefit: they're usually available for free from a family with post-infant children, or for very little money from the Salvation Army, a Goodwill store, or hospital outpatient department.

Professional scales may be used, but their cost would likely make them prohibitive. However, a watchful eye for going-out-of-business sales and wholesale and retail equipment clearances could net a perfect one cheaply.

I do not recommend bathroom scales, although some people use them. They tend to be less accurate to the pound than the other types mentioned. Bathroom scales seldom carry ounce-by-ounce markings.

A used refrigerator can be a real blessing to a new co-op if it would be an aid in making some of the purchasing choices. Any member willing to donate one should be the object of gratitude. Or, a second-hand store, rummage sale or auction could yield one. The refrigerator need not have a freezer, all its shelving, or a paint job. Besides home refrigerators, consider small commercial models a going-out-of-business grocer might have, or even a florist's chiller case.

Smaller items, such as a broom, dustpan, mop, pencils, marking pens, tape, scissors, cheese-cutting knife, used egg cartons and paper bags, should also be kept on your equipment and supplies list.

The backs of old correspondence, press releases or

business-trade mailings should be the co-op's source of paper for notes and tabulating scratch paper.

Never buy anything that the co-op needs that can be secured free of charge by one of the members. To ensure this, always let everyone know what the co-op needs. (The order form is the best method of reaching each and every member with such an announcement or a notice.)

Place and Space A sense of fairness and an eagerness to parcel out the burdens equitably among all the members may prompt a suggestion that the food be distributed from a different member's home each time you shop. I advise against this proposal for the following reasons.

1) Not all homes are equipped to handle the operations that will take place at the distribution center (see the checklist on p. 88 of what your eventual space should contain).

2) When and if you develop a relationship with a wholesaler who will deliver goods to you, a permanent address is virtually a necessity. (Such a wholesaler is a blessing, especially if your group isn't situated in an inner-urban area.) The last thing you'll want to do is trouble a delivery person with a new location each time you order.

3) If you decide on certain occasions to overorder some items like rice, molasses, onions, black-eyed peas, or peanut butter in order to reach a bulk amount, the decision may be made with the idea of storing the surplus for a few weeks and offering it for sale again. A permanent location facilitates this plan.

4) The distribution equipment, such as scales, bags of all sizes, egg cartons, knife, pencils, etc., are all better stationed at one place rather than shuffled from place to place.

5) Your group may decide, as most do, to sell surplus food at a markup after all members' orders have been filled. If the distribution center remains in one place, nonmembers in the immediate vicinity become regular customers for this left-over food. For instance, a co-op might have a few pounds of apples, some tomatoes, and an extra head of cabbage left after all the orders have been filled. Neighbors living on the same street or in the same apartment building might be invited to come and purchase these leftovers during an hour period after regular members have taken their choices.

6) Your calculations on the costs of gas, oil, and tolls paid

to the driver/shopper could be more or less standardized if the trip always covers approximately the same distance.

All the above doesn't mean there are any firm rules about distribution location. Many co-ops float it each time, every other time, or every fourth time they shop. My recommendations concerning distribution centers is based on the above reasons, plus a belief that however loosely a group decides to run things, some regular features will provide a structural core that will keep the other constantly shifting elements together.

Here are the features to look for and some considerations to weigh in siting your distribution center:

1) Large enough to handle boxes, crates, baskets, and bunches of foods. These food containers won't remain stacked; they'll be shifted, lifted, dropped, opened, emptied, stepped over, and walked around. There must also be room for one or two grocery bags for each member of the group, because at midpoint in some systems of distribution, all the bags and all the food containers will be half full and lying on the floor or on countertops.

2) Sheltered enough not to be affected by adverse weather. A porch, yard, or patio may do very well most of the year in certain regions, but be ready with an indoor alternative in case of rain.

3) Well lit, to make reading of small numbers and mimeographed sheets as easy as possible. You must remember that all ages of people may join, and older folks may have weaker eyes and need more light.

4) An easily cleaned floor, to compensate for the inevitable stray lettuce leaves, turnip tops, and ice sometimes used to pack vegetables. Also, there's the occasional broken bottle of mayonnaise or eggs. A ready access to water will prove helpful.

(A note on garbage: some municipalities may balk at what appears to be commercial trash put out for regular pickup. You can help alleviate this potential conflict if you disassemble all cardboard cartons by pulling apart the bottom flaps. No tearing is necessary. Flatten the cardboard and place it inside the largest crate, which has been left intact. Consolidate all empty non-reusable bags, sacks, egg separators, papers, and other packing materials into one container, thereby reducing to two or three pieces the garbage your co-op generates. Of course, let anyone who wants to reclaim some of those sturdy vegetable cartons, the handy mushroom baskets and strawberry trays, the egg separators commonly used for insulation, the wooden-slatted crates which hold record albums so trimly, or any other container they choose to recycle. If any member whose business uses a commercial pickup offers to help, place the garbage with his nearby commercial trash for pickup.)

5) Working with scales moves much more smoothly when you can weigh out the goods at waist level. For this, a counter-top surface is ideal. But an abandoned card table, workbench, television console, bureau, or two dining-room chairs with a board across the top will serve admirably, so long as the surface is steady and can hold the scales. Cover the surface with newspaper or waxed paper to protect it and ease clean-up.

6) Choose a location that could serve your group even if it doubles in size. This is, of course, not a primary requirement, but if you've gone through the trouble of creating a comfortable, suitable distribution center, you'll feel better about the arrival of new members if they don't bring with them the need for the co-op to find a larger space.

7) Access to the distribution center is crucial. Foods, usually heavy, must be unloaded and carried into this work area. Try to find a street-level place, or one at basement level, so that heavy (50–100 pound) bulk containers, when purchased, are carried downstairs into the distribution center—it's easier for each member to carry smaller bags of groceries up that flight of stairs.

Also, access to the place itself must be considered. A public area, such as an apartment building lobby or a church vestibule, encounters other foot traffic, and you must allow for that non co-op traffic to pass freely. Members stopping by for their food should not have to park cars several blocks away, either. Remember that in some cases a parent must pick up the household's food while leaving a child or children in a car parked some distance away. Even without this problem, a few blocks would be too far to walk carrying several bundles.

8) In regions that enjoy seasonal weather, some sort of heating during cold months is highly recommended.

9) If the group decides on a refrigerator for dairy or meat items, an electrical outlet is, of course, essential.

10) If you plan to store your equipment, as well as any surplus food, at the distribution center, you must make sure that it can be securely locked.

Food

The Co-op's Food Needs

It is important to use an organized method for selecting the foods to buy which will fulfill the different needs of each member. If your group is small enough (six to ten people), and already knows each other very well (members of the same family, for example), a long talk-session might well produce a consensus of which foods to begin with. This method is perfectly acceptable as long as everyone in the co-op is present when it takes place and there's plenty of time to discuss the choices thoughtfully.

If this is not the case, there are two basic systems that can be used for determining food items the group should purchase.

The Big Checklist system: As many people as are interested leaf through cookbooks or recipe files to compile a long list of all kinds of foods they could conceivably want. A master food list is then made from the compilation of all the smaller ones. Each member gets a copy of this list, and indicates on it a preference for or against the items. Those foods which receive the greatest tally are then considered the ones most likely to garner bulk orders from your group time after time and the ones the co-op should try to buy wholesale.

The list could also ask members to indicate the number of pounds or pieces they use each week. For example, a household that uses five oranges a week would vote "5" for oranges, and would vote "zero" for limes if none are used. A two-pound-per-week cheese order would receive a "2" vote.

Your group may wish to indicate their choices directly on one central list kept at someone's home rather than preparing copies of the Big Checklist. It could be done at a central meeting, over the telephone, or in person during a several-day stretch. If some members don't trust others enough to indicate their choices by phone, your group is not ready to run a food co-op; trust is an integral part of any co-op venture. If you decide to do this at a general meeting, allow plenty of time, because each person must be as accurate as possible in recording his food preferences.

The Two-Week Menu Survey system: Each member keeps paper and a pencil in the kitchen. For two weeks, a listing of the foods and the amounts consumed is made after each meal; snacks and sandwiches, as well as non-group meals (breakfast and lunch in many homes), are also carefully recorded, either by the preparer or the eater.

This system takes a little longer (two weeks represents a time period during which an average range of foods is consumed) and involves a bit more time and effort on everyone's part, but it provides the group with a more accurate recording of the foods each household is likely to order.

Don't include holiday or traditional once-a-year dishes in the two-week menu survey.

In either system, be certain that members don't select foods they've never used but would like to try. These "wish foods" may eventually wind up on your list and your table from time to time as people develop a willingness to experiment with a new item now and then. But this step should be reserved for the future. If your goal is a stable, soundly organized and smoothly run co-op, stick strictly to the daily favorites that you know the group will order regularly.

Either system will reveal the kinds of foods your group buys for everyday use. When you tabulate the totals, it's not necessary to note which households represent which foods and in what amounts. Only the totals are important.

If your group happens to need almost exactly the same types and amounts of foods week in and week out, you will need to determine only the amounts. For example, a day-care center kitchen staff that serves the same basic two-week pattern of lunches, or a religious, spiritual or other group with a rigid set of eating habits and one central kitchen for meals for all its members, would have no need to draw up a list of choices.

Whatever the case, be certain that no decision to research prices and suppliers for specific items is made until each member has had a chance to express an opinion and to vote on what foods he wants the co-op to buy. Remember that all through the research and set-up stages, each member must feel that she or he has an opportunity to take part in every decision.

After either the Big Checklist or the Two-Week Menu Survey system has been completed, you should have an indication of which foods your co-op is interested in buying and hopefully some information on the quantity of each item the total group requires.

Group the foods into categories by kind of food—fruits, vegetables, eggs, cheeses and other dairy products, meats, fish, baked goods, dried foods and grains, condiments, beverages— and by the form in which they arrive in the kitchen—fresh, canned, frozen or prepackaged. Some foods, such as carrots can be obtained fresh, canned, etc., whereas eggs are generally only sold fresh.

Eliminate from this giant list those items that received only minimal support. Exceptions, such as instances when one or two households could absorb bulk orders for a particular item, may be folded into the operation after only two weeks' time. For now, it's best to keep the list as broadly based as possible.

Then eliminate any items that are sold close to wholesale cost at markets. Most canned goods fall into this category. And the overhead (freezer units) of dealing in bulk amounts of frozen foods will probably cause those items to be dropped, at least for now.

In its earliest stages, your co-op should handle foods that provide the greatest bulk order, realize the highest percentage of savings and are available from wholesalers for co-op purchase.

Availability of the remaining items should now be researched. You should retain as many items as possible from the trimmed list for this wholesale supply research stage, since half may not be available, or available only seasonably, or may not represent a financial savings even if they are available. This will give you a substantial number of choices from which to compile your first order form.

Some members may be concerned or interested to learn about government standards or grades of foods. For more information on this subject, see Appendix C.

What Foods Are Available

Finding sources of supply for the foods your co-op wants is the next task, and there are several methods for locating them. Wholesale outlets of foods are easiest to find in urban locations, because obviously the greater concentration of people requires more food sources. But if your co-op is in a rural area, keep in mind that local supermarkets, grocery stores, hotels and motels, restaurants, schools, institutions with cafeterias and lunch programs, hospitals, bakeries—all these and more—require wholesale distributors to service them and often enjoy the benefit of delivery to regular bulk-order customers. Your combined co-op order for eggs and cheese may equal that of a small corner restaurant or grocery store; if it's half their order, you may need to deal with the wholesaler only half as frequently.

The Yellow Pages list wholesale food distributors in all areas under such headings as:

Bakers' Suppliers

Bakers—Wholesale

Dairy Products Brokers

Eggs, Cheese, Butter

Food Brokers

Food Products—Manufacturers and Distributors

Fruits and Vegetables—Wholesale

Grocers—Wholesale

Health Food Products—Wholesalers/Manufacturers

Meat, Wholesale

Milk and Milk Products

Natural Foods

Nuts, Edible—Wholesale

Oils, Vegetable

Poultry—Wholesale

Restaurant Purveyors

Sugar Brokers and Wholesalers

Cooks, nutritionists or members of the above-mentioned institutional kitchen staffs (or their friends) should be able to tell you their suppliers' names and addresses. Assure them that you will keep your contact with them strictly confidential if they wish it.

Anyone with a flexible schedule can observe what goes on

at a few grocery stores for a couple of days and simply jot down the names and addresses on the sides of vans or trucks as they make their deliveries.

Most sources of fresh produce in city or large-town regions will be situated at the closest terminal market or wholesale food district. If you're not sure exactly where it is, you might be able to detect a pattern from the Yellow Pages listings: see if half or more of the addresses are in the same general area. All information dealing with that area of purchasing is given in this section.

Finally, a very, very important and wise consideration: make every effort to contact area farmers directly. Your local or regional branch office of the Department of Agriculture might help. Or else post a sign at stores where farmers would shop for supplies; ask regional 4-H Club leaders for help; Future Farmers of America might supply some names. Dealing with farmers would give them a friendly, direct market and give you a friendly, minimal markup. You'd be supporting a small operation which may be facing the threat of losing its holdings if forced to accept corporate prices for crops; by selling to people close by, the farmer could get a price higher than the corporate price, and the co-op could get a price lower than the wholesale price. And you'd know exactly where some of your food is coming from.

Approaching wholesalers brings you into contact with a wide variety of people. Some are producer-distributors, who know everything about their food products because they produce them. Most, though, are first- or second-level middlemen who could just as easily be dealing in wallets as walnuts.

Pricing A phone call to the ordering department of many suppliers and distributors should result in a catalog or price list. (Don't tell them the size of your co-op; hint that it's large, but new.) Do not expect to do extensive research by telephone. Wholesale distributors not operating at a terminal market conduct a large portion of their business transactions by phone, and you'll create a negative first impression for your group if you begin by asking lots of questions during business hours. After you've received whatever list they have by mail, call and ask for an appointment with a salesperson.

Produce distributors cannot supply pricing information to you, but a very good estimate of current pricing rates is obtainable. Write to the closest office of the Department of Agriculture, listing your co-op's name and an address where the co-op receives mail. Request their *Fresh Fruits and Vegetable Market News* of available produce for the nearest terminal market. This bulletin, available in a daily or weekly version, is published with tax money, and should be free of charge for the asking.

In researching what foods are available and their costs, you need to learn several things from the distributors. These include:

1) The smallest bulk order they will handle (don't, however, give the impression you'll only be dealing in the smallest).

2) The bulk quantities the foods they handle come in.

3) Days of the week and hours of the day they're open.

4) Whether they do a cash-only business, check-only business, or both.

5) Whether and under what conditions they deliver.

6) Whether orders must be prepaid.

7) If they handle quantities large enough to assure you that no pre-ordering by telephone is necessary, or whether you need to phone in orders before you wish to pick them up, and how long in advance this call must be placed.

8) Under what circumstances and when do they accept goods back for a refund or for future credit.

9) What methods of obtaining information on price changes and new items offered they use to keep customers up-to-date.

How to Buy Produce

An exploratory trip to the closest wholesale terminal market should be scheduled very soon. Plan for a few people to make the trip so that the sense of what goes on there can be experienced and shared firsthand by as many members as possible. You should arrive there no later than 5 or 5:30 A.M., when most of the business is transacted, for the real day-to-day feel of the place.

When you arrive, you may have to pay an entrance fee (major city markets have a collection station similar to a highway toll booth setup); the fee per vehicle is nominal—perhaps 50 cents. Once your group begins shopping there regularly it may want to purchase a window sticker, decal or special pass for a few dollars, good for one year. Also, you can then use the regular customers' lane, and not wait in the "pay lane." Smaller markets may not require a fee of any amount.

Park in the designated area only and walk around from stall to stall, watching how the actual process of purchasing occurs. Many stalls will be selling the same produce items and competing with each other. For example, some stalls may be selling all citrus, or all fruits from one region of the country, or all small vegetables; some may have most available produce items. The easiest method, of course, would be to stop at the first stall and do all your buying if it happens to have everything you need, but you will want to get the best bargains. After all, that's one of the reasons the co-op was established. When you actually begin to buy at a wholesale market remember that your shoppers must be urged to compare price *and* quality at various stalls, and then do their selective purchasing. It may seem a bit overwhelming at the outset, with legions of bright purple eggplant, plump red strawberries, crisp green Chinese cabbages, voluminous watermelons and pungent limes all bidding for your attention. But keep your eyes open and take in all that's going on.

Buyers (from retail markets, restaurants, institutions, and co-ops) approach the person called the seller (or in some instances the dispatcher), who is usually seated at a desk or table at the front of the stall or selling area. This person has a large graphlike chart that resembles a scorecard, which shows the seller at a glance what amounts are left in stock, and to whom he has already sold food. The seller may be walking around, and may have this chart located at a desk or in a booth inside the stall. Buyers ask about prices of specific items in specific quantities, for example, yams in a 50-pound sack. If they decide to buy, the seller issues them a ticket or voucher. Note that buyers generally wait their turn in line and do not attempt to force their questions or orders on the seller. Make this professional courtesy a built-in practice for anyone who shops for the co-op.

The ticket lists the item, the quantity, the cost, the order number, and the buyer. Sometimes a code name is used to designate the buyer. (The Broadway Local sometimes uses "Natalie," the name of one of the women who played an active part in the setting up of the co-op at its beginning, and used to do much of the shopping then). The seller then charts what's been sold, and deals with the next buyer in line.

Next stop for the buyer is the cashier for the stall. This person usually only takes the money and validates the ticket. Then the loading foreman takes over. His job is to coordinate the work of the loading crew, which handles the picking up of the order from within the stall and the carting of the order to the buyer's vehicle. This is done in the sequence the loading foreman receives the tickets from buyers. Sometimes, if a buyer is in an unusual hurry, he can ask the loading foreman if the order could be filled sooner. This should not be a common practice. The loading foreman will or will not comply, depending on how flexible his routine is, and how pleasant his mood is.

The buyer then makes it clear exactly where his or her vehicle is parked. A very wise practice is for someone to remain with the vehicle at all times, since it must be open and accessible for the loading crew members. It is at this point, when the food is delivered to the co-op's shopping vehicle, that the food should be checked for freshness, and to be certain it is exactly what has been paid for, as stated on the receipt (not Bibb lettuce instead of romaine, not Temple oranges instead of tangelos, etc.). If for any reason the food is not what it should be, it can be refused and sent back with the loading crew and the proper items redelivered. If there's any question about whether the loading crew will follow these instructions, someone can accompany them back to the wholesale stall area where the loading foreman works.

In smaller operations, the cashier and the loading foreman may be the same person.

Once the buyer returns to the distribution center and the food is unloaded, some spoiled produce may be discovered with the other goods—not simply a random couple of bad oranges in two boxes, or a bad stalk of celery, but an entire bad carton. If that happens, the buyer calls the seller at once, explains what happened, and tells him how much is bad and what was paid for it. Usually, the damaged goods will have to be returned for credit or replacement. In some cases, either after repeated business dealings or if the wholesaler really values the co-op's business very highly, the co-op can negotiate a partial credit over the phone and not return the item; the credit can then be used during the next shopping trip. All this emphasizes the importance of checking the foods while they are being loaded into the shopping vehicle in the parking lot of the terminal market.

After a few members have visited the wholesale produce market, these additional points should be kept in mind:

1) Arriving early means bargains and best quality; the later shoppers arrive at the market, the more likely they are to be left with poorer quality to choose from. Early arrival means no later than 5 A.M. or 5:30 A.M.

2) In the beginning—and in some cases always—buying fresh produce is a cash transaction business. It's important then to send someone who is naturally careful with money. Because prices are almost always rounded off to the nearest 50 cents or 25 cents, the shoppers do not usually need to carry change with them.

3) Sellers operate on a first come, first serve basis. They also respond well to shoppers who know what they want and are decisive. (It follows, therefore, that they're less than pleased with shoppers who know nothing and can't make up their minds.) This does not mean that you have to be worried about being new; just try to learn as much as you can in advance, and once you've found what you want to buy, buy it, and don't waste the time of the seller or the other people in the buying line.

4) If the co-op wants to buy one batch of large grocery bags and then recycle them within the co-op, sellers can usually be found handling them at the terminal market. They generally come in packages of 250.

Wholesale Produce Market

To make your overall learning process easier and less time-consuming, a brief description of what to look for in fresh fruits and vegetables follows.

Also, the accompanying list gives the usual wholesale containers that produce is packaged in. Exceptions do occur, especially if you're dealing with local farmers, but by and large, these containers and quantities are the nationally utilized standard sizes.

Remember that "bushel" is a volume measurement, and by itself does not tell you either how many of something is in the container or how much it weighs. If other terms in this listing are unfamiliar or unclear, consult the Glossary.

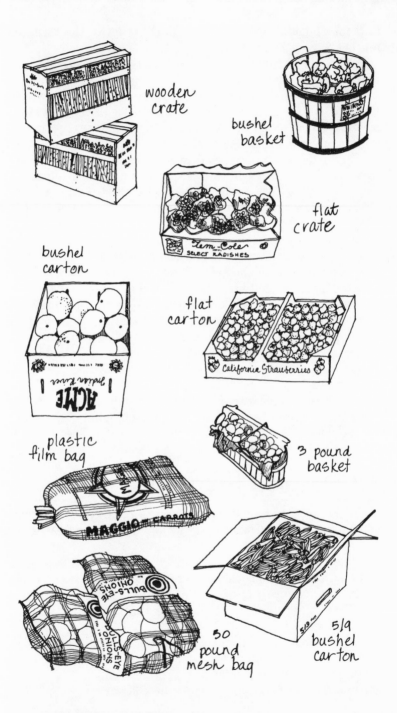

wooden crate

bushel basket

flat crate

bushel carton

flat carton

plastic film bag

3 pound basket

50 pound mesh bag

5/9 bushel carton

bushel
hamper

bunched

crate
by count

crate

1 1/9 bushel
carton

carton
packed by
weight

The first test of freshness for any item of produce is its smell. Never be afraid or hesitant about sniffing the food you are about to buy. An off-smell will signal you to stay away. Apply this test across the board to all fresh fruits and vegetables, regardless of any other tests or signs you look for.

Apples

Yellow Transparent	clear, yellow skin; sweet taste
Delicious	red or yellow skin; bumps on bottom (picture book apples); sweet
McIntosh	thin-skinned, red and some green when ripe; tangy taste
Jonathan	deep red color; eating apples
Winesap	dark red color; tart; cooking apples
Granny Smiths	hard; sprightly taste; cooking or eating
Rome Beauties	bright-red color; cooking
Cortland	like McIntosh; may be tart

Sold in cartons by count (80–120); buy fresh-picked; ask for local apples; avoid soft, spotted or overripe apples

Artichokes

French or *Globe*	plump, substantial globes; green fleshy leaves; medium and large size are best

Sold in flat cartons of 20, 48, 54, and 72; avoid withered, spotted or spreading leaves, or brownish-colored globes

Jerusalem	smooth texture

Sold in flat cartons of 12 one-pound packages; avoid discolored, spotted, or bruised ones

Asparagus

	should be firm and tender; small or medium-sized are best; tips should be tight; uniform green color

Sold by weight in cartons; avoid brownish or yellowish spotted, wilted appearance, tough stalks, or spreading tips

Avocadoes

hard, green, fairly firm; medium and large sizes are best buys

Sold in cartons, usually 14 per; avoid those that are soft or have black spots or dots, bruised or broken skins

Bananas

buy green, which allows 4–5 days to ripen; maximum 9″ in length; don't buy ripe bananas

Sold in 40-pound cartons; avoid overripe, those that are too long, or have broken skins

Beans

String or *Snap*   should snap when broken; very firm; mild green color

Pole   more rugged than snap beans; find ones with full pods

Sold in bushel crates of 28–30 pounds; avoid limp, soft, discolored, wilted, tough, dirty, or blemished beans

Beets

round, firm, large bottoms; buy with full tops, which can be cooked as greens

Sold by crate, 35–45 pounds; avoid those that are cracked, soft or spongy, or shriveled

Broccoli

deep green in color; tight buds; try for few leaves; may be hard to test for tenderness because often packed in ice

Sold in cartons, usually about 20 pounds; avoid yellow stalks, wilted leaves, tough stalks

Brussels Sprouts

light green color; firm; uniform size

Sold in flat cartons, usually with twelve 10-ounce cardboard cups in each; avoid yellow or worm-holed leaves, brownness, wilted leaves

Cabbage

Head   heavy; crisp leaves; uniform color; large heads are best buy

Sold in crates of 12–18 per, totaling 50 or 75 pounds; avoid brown or yellow edges on leaves, wilted or soft leaves

Chinese   firm; looks like cross between romaine and celery

Sold in bushel crates of 28–30 pounds; avoid wilted or soft, or discolored leaves

Carrots

firm; smooth; bright orange; may have green near tops; leaves can be eaten;

Sold unbunched in multipound bags; sold in large film bags containing 48 one-pound bags; avoid those that are cracked, tough, wilted, soft or discolored

Cauliflower

firm; tight buds or flowerettes; white color; compact bunches

Sold in flat cartons of 12 or 16; avoid yellow or brown spots or edges, loose flowerettes, wilted or yellowing leaves, loose bunches

Celery

firm, brittle; breaks crisply; sharp green and white color; fresh leaves

Sold in crates and cartons of 1, 1½, 2 and 2½ dozen; avoid stalks that are bruised, brown or yellow, wilted, soft, or too leafy

Chicory

curly, narrow leaves; slightly bitter; resembles romaine lettuce; crisp; loose head

Sold in bushel crates, about 20 pounds per; avoid wilted, brown, tough leaves

Collards

dark green; crisp

Sold in bushel crates, weight varies; avoid wilted, yellowing, or leaves with holes

Corn

bright green husks; plump ears; mature corn has brown silks coming out of top of ears; check for full kernels

Sold 48 ears to crate; avoid husks that are brittle, dry, yellow or have worm holes or rotted spots

Cucumbers

all green skin; firm; medium size is best; slightly textured skin no problem

Sold 70–90 per carton; avoid those that are mushy, whitish, or shriveled

Dandelion

fresh green in color; tender leaves

Sold in bushel crates; weight varies; avoid tough, wilted, or discolored leaves

Eggplant

uniform dark, purple skin; tight firm top leaves hugging sides; heavy, shiny; some find lighter eggplant sweeter

Sold in cartons of 24–32 per; avoid those that are spotted, soft, or shriveled

Escarole

broad, spiky twisted, tender leaves; color goes from dark green to white

Sold about 24 heads to a bushel crate; avoid wilted; rotting or off-color

Fennel (Finocchio)

large round bottom bulbs; bright green tops; anise taste

Sold crated, weight varies; avoid spotted, rotting, yellowing

Garlic

dry-skinned; solid; plump

Sold in cartons of 48 to 57 bulbs each; also in film bags of various weights; avoid broken or cracked, soft, or sprouted bulbs

Grapefruit

large size is best buy; firm

Sold in bushel cartons from 23 to 48 per; avoid bruised, mushy fruit

Kale

crisp; dark green color (may tend to look brownish in winter season)

Sold in bushel carton, weight varies from 20 to 30 pounds; avoid yellow or wilted leaves; these greens are sometimes carriers of plant lice, so examine each carton carefully

Leeks

dark green tops; whitish stalks and bulbs; fairly crisp or firm

Sold 12 bunches to a bushel crate; avoid blemished, wilted, yellowing, broken or cracked stalks

Lemons

larger fruit are more juicy; firm

Sold in cartons of 115, 140 and 165; avoid old, tough fruit; one rotten lemon can damage the rest

Lettuce

Bibb	small heads; deep rich green color; leafy
Boston	round leaves, dark green, firm hard heads, very perishable; heaviest heads are best buy
Crisphead, or *Iceberg*	watery crisp leaves; tight head, greenish white color
Leaf Type	light green, spiky leaves
Romaine	dark green that moderates to light green at stalk; long leaves; sweet

Sold 24 to a bushel; avoid wilted, yellowing, or rust-tipped leaves

Limes

full, plump feel (squeeze them); color may be yellowish instead of green

Sold in 10-pound cartons of about 42 to 54 each, and 20-pound cartons of about 126 each; avoid shriveled or shrunken fruit

Melons

firm; top should yield to pressure of two fingers; solid

Sold in cartons with from 5 to 12 each; avoid soft, mushy fruit

Mushrooms

white; underside of caps should not show separation from stem; firm caps and stems; tiny ones are tender but hard to slice

Sold in flat trays of 8 one-pound packages, or in 3-pound baskets; avoid spotted, moldy, shriveled, or broken skins, or flabby or woody stems

Nectarines

firm, hard; will ripen quickly; should look like a hairless peach

Sold in 2-layer crate, with 22-pounds each crate; avoid soft, overripe fruit

Okra

firm; green or white color; should have a crisp snap when broken

Sold in bushel crates, about 40 pounds per; may vary in weight of crates; avoid dried-out, shriveled, or off-color pods

Onions

Dry   should be hard when squeezed; dry outer skins; large size is more economical; Purple Bermudas are sweet; red and white onions are not

Sold in 50-pound sacks; avoid those that are mushy, sprouting, or bruised; check for moisture near top of onion (should be dry)

Scallions   bright green stems and tops; white bulbs

Sold in crates, 60–80 bunches per; avoid wilted, yellowing tops and damaged bulbs

Oranges

Blood	deep red streaks in juicy pulp; few seeds
Juice	thin-skinned, not very large, seedy; may be irregular in shape
Navel	seedless; thick skins; have navel for peeling; bright color may be due to dyes or artificial coloring
Tangelos	cross between oranges and tangerines
Tangerines	should peel fairly easily; somewhat firm; avoid too soft fruit

Other orange varieties may be common in various parts of the country

Sold in cartons of 88, 100, 120, and 140; avoid spotted or soft fruit; ask for freshest shipment; color may be deceptive, since ripe oranges can be green or orange/brown

Parsley

uniform green; crisp

Sold usually in bushel crates of 5 dozen bunches each; avoid wilted, yellowing leaves

Parsnips

smooth-skinned; medium size is best; firm

Sold in 25-pound film bags; avoid those that are soft, too large, shriveled or spotted

Peas

tender, sweet taste; plump full pods; smooth skins

Sold in bushel crates or bushel hampers—weight varies; avoid wilted, splitting, wet, or rotting pods, or pods with fading color

Peaches

firm and hard; buy to ripen at home

Sold in ½ bushel basket, about 23 pounds per; avoid those that are soft or wet, or have bruised or broken skins

Pears

firm and smooth skins

Sold in crates by count—number varies; avoid soft, bruised, or broken skins; avoid spots or worm damage; expensive out-of-season

Peppers, Green Bell

shiny green color; uniform shape; thick-skinned; firm to the touch

Sold in bushel crates and cartons—weight varies; avoid soft spots, broken skins, brown or black spots

Pineapples

should be solid; test for freshness by picking up pineapple by topmost leaf (spiky); if fresh, leaf will break off

Sold 12 to 15 in a carton; avoid those that are soft or fail freshness test

Plantains (Platinos)

bright green color; firm; length not a problem

Sold in 40-pound cartons; avoid those that are soft or have black spotted skin

Potatoes

Sweet	pink or white color (see **Yams** to learn difference); firm; not excessively spotted, but may have freckles here and there; plump

Sold in 50-pound cartons; avoid those with soft spots or roots remaining, or those that are damp or moist, or have large black areas

White	should be firm to the touch; no sprouting eyes

Sold in 50-pound bags or sacks; avoid those that are mushy or soft, or have broken wilted, or shriveled skins; may be sold unwashed

Radishes

Red or *White*	hard; white or red uniform color; red should be small, white medium; crisp leaves; should be firm

Sold in cartons with 30 six-ounce bags, or 24 bunches to a crate, and in other amounts; avoid soft, spongy, bruised or broken; avoid roots

Spinach

crisp leaves; bushy heads; dark green

Sold in bushel baskets, 20–25 pounds per; avoid wilted, off-color leaves or stems and woody, tough veins or stems

Squash

Acorn	dark green and yellow; very hard shell
Butternut	light brown, creamy yellow color; smooth-skinned; heavy; fingernail should puncture skin

*Other squash varieties common in various parts
of the country*

Sold in 40-pound bushels; avoid those that are bruised or have
soft spots and blemished skin with wrong texture

Strawberries

---

                         firm; beginning to turn full red, may
have white areas; plump; medium size is
generally best, but large is also good

Sold in flat cartons of 12 one-pint containers or baskets; avoid
wet, soft, mushy, too ripe fruit or rotten ones at bottom; seller
may shake basket to create air pockets in baskets, so be
sure basket is filled with berries, not air

Tomatoes

Red or Yellow   buy vine-ripened for best quality; find
green and hard, allow them to ripen at
home; should be smooth-skinned

Sold in 20-pound and 30-pound cartons; avoid cracked skin,
bruised or soft spots or overripeness; be certain tomatoes do not
freeze during winter, because they will ripen slower or not at
all; even very cold temperatures will retard their ripening and
the filling in of true color

Turnips

White and *Yellow*
  (Rutabagas)   both should be smooth-skinned, with
even texture, and roots removed; whites
should still have tops (edible) and leaves
should be crisp, tender

Sold in 25-pound film bags, and in bushel crates with varying
amounts of bunches; avoid those with soft spots or are wrinkled
or too large; puncture with fingernail—if dry inside, turnip
is probably overripe or stringy

Watercress

dark green color; crisp, tender, tangy leaves; perishes quickly so get freshest shipment

Sold in lots of 12 bunches; avoid wilted, rusted, or yellowing leaves or very small leaves with lots of stems

Watermelon

white of the rind should be as narrow as possible (seller will have to cut one open to show you); should be fresh

Sold in various sizes and quantities; avoid old ones (bargains are likely to be old and ripening fast) and those with soft spots

Yams

not the same as sweet potatoes (see **Potatoes,** *Sweet*)—yams are orange or darker red in color; and should be more crescent-shaped than sweet potatoes; firm; no large dark spots

Sold in 50-pound sacks or in cartons; avoid soft spots, blemishes, broken skins, root growth

Zucchini

should be narrow; dark green, no yellow; medium-size is best buy; should be firm if squeezed

Sold in 30-pound cartons and various weight bushels; avoid those with soft spots or have wrinkled blemished skin or are extra large or too small

Fresh Fruit and Vegetable Market News

The Department of Agriculture's *Fresh Fruit and Vegetable Market News* is printed in code, primarily because of space problems, but partly because it is a copy of reports transmitted by wire from all regions of the country. To aid you in decoding this jumble of letters, numbers and phrases, here's a list of the common abbreviations used, and their meanings:

ABSTDY	About Steady	CULT	Cultivated
APL	Apple	CUX	Cucumbers
APPROX	Approximately	DAND	Dandelion
APR	Apricot	DECID	Deciduous
ART	Artichoke	DIR RCT	Direct Receipt
AVOC	Avocado	STSLS	Street Sales
BCHD	Bunched	DIST	District
BKT	Basket	DOMRND	Domestic
BLD	Baled		Round Type
BLK	Black	DZ	Dozen
BLUBY	Blueberry	EBNCRT	Eastern Boston
BNS	Beans		Crate
BRND	Brand	EGPLT	Eggplant
BROC	Broccoli	ENDV	Endive
BTS	Beets	ESC	Escarole
BUBKT	Bushel Basket	EXFLR	Extra Flower
BUCTN	Bushel Carton	FCY	Fancy
BUCRT	Bushel Crate	FHIAS	Few High As
BUHPR	Bushel Hamper	FLM MSTR	Film Master
BX	Box	FLMW	Film Wrapped
CAB	Cabbage	FLR	Flower
CANT	Cantaloupe	FLMC	Film Covered
CAUL	Cauliflower	FLT	Flat
CEL	Celery	FLCRT	Flat Crate
CELPK	Cellophane	FLCTN	Flat Carton
	Pack	FLWR	Few Lower
CHER	Cherry	FRC	Fair Condition
CHCAB	Chinese	FRQ	Fair Quality
	Cabbage	GARL	Garlic
COLL	Collards	GEN	Generally
CASTAGE	Controlled	GD	Good
	Atmosphere	GLB	Globe Tray
COND	Condition	GRD	Grade
CNTNL	Centennial	GRN	Green
CNTR	Container	GRNHSE	Greenhouse
CRAN	Cranshaw	GRPS	Grapes
CRBY	Cranberry	GRPFT	Grapefruit
CRT	Crate	HDEW	Honeydew
CTN	Carton	HGR	Higher
CWDR	California	HIAS	High As
	Wonder Type	HLDVR	Holdover

IB	Iceberg Type
INC	Incomplete
INCL	Including
INSUFQ	Insufficient Supplies to Quote
INT	Interior
IRREG	Irregular
ITAL	Italian
JBO	Jumbo
LB	Pound
LEM	Lemon
LETT	Lettuce
LGE	Large
LGR	Larger
LGT	Light
LICRT	Long Island Type Cauliflower Crate
LIM	Limes
LOAS	Low As
LSE	Loose
LWR	Lower
LYR	Layer
MED	Medium
MIN	Minimum
MKT	Market
MSTLY	Mostly
MSTRC	Master Container
MUSH	Mushroom
MUST	Mustard
MXD	Mixed
MXD CITRUS	Mixed Citrus
MXD DECID	Mixed Deciduous
MXD MEL	Mixed Melon
MXD VEG	Mixed Vegetable
NECT	Nectarines
NOGRDMK	No Grade Mark
NTHG GD OFD	Nothing Good Offered
NTHG OFD	Nothing Offered
OCC	Occasional
OFD	Offered
OFS	Offerings
ORD	Ordinary
ORG	Oranges
OTHR	Other
OVRP	Over-Ripe
OVRWRPD	Over-Wrapped
OZ	Ounce
PARSL	Parsley
PARSN	Parsnips
PCH	Peaches
PEP	Peppers
PERS	Persians
PK	Pack
PKG	Package
PLN	Plain
POTS	Potatoes
PRR	Poorer
PUN	Previously Unreported
PRECEX	Precooling Extra
QT	Quart
QUAL	Quality
RAD	Radishes
RCT	Receipt
RHUB	Rhubarb
RND	Round
RNDRD	Round Red Type
RNDWH	Round White Type
RPTD	Reported
R-T	Rail-Truck
RUS	Russet
RUT	Rutabagas
SAV	Savoy
SCLAUS	Santa Claus
SECT	Section
SHWG	Showing
SK	Sack
SLS	Sales
SLSTGR	Slightly Stronger
SLWKR	Slightly Weaker

SML	Small	USONE	U.S. Grade
SPEC	Special		One
SPIN	Spinach	USXFCY	U.S. Extra
SQU	Squash		Fancy
STDY	Steady	CUSXFF	Combination
STGR	Stronger		U.S. Extra
STRBY	Strawberries		Fancy, Fancy
STSLS	Street Sales	VAR	Variety
SWPOT	Sweet Potatoes	VLY	Valley
SZ	Size	VVAR	Various
SZD	Sized		Varieties
TANG	Tangerines	WBCRT	Wirebound
TOM	Tomatoes	WDFLT	Wood Flat
TPD	Topped	WHBLR	White Boiler
TRAPK	Tray Pack	WKR	Weaker
TURN	Turnips	WMEL	Watermelon
TURNTOPS	Turnip Tops	WRPD	Wrapped
UNOWST	Unless Other-	WSHD	Washed
	wise Stated	WXD	Waxed
UNWSHD	Unwashed	XFCY	Extra Fancy
USCOML	U.S.	XGIANT	Extra Giant
	Commercial	XJBO	Extra Jumbo
USFCY	U.S. Fancy	XLGE	Extra Large

Nearly all the abbreviations are self-explanatory. Some that need clarification are Steady or Strong, which relate to price fluctuations—"strong" means prices are rising; "weak" means prices are going down and "steady" means steady prices. Don't assume an abbreviation means something unless you've checked it with the list. For example, you may think FRQ is Frequently, when in fact it stands for Fair Quality.

Additionally, state-name abbreviations are used to indicate fruit and vegetable points of origin. These abbreviations are the same as the U.S. Post Office Zip Code abbreviations, with the following additions: CA (California, North); CC (California, Central); CF (California, South); CI (California, Imperial Valley; DC (District of Columbia); YY (Unknown); ZZ (Imports) usually, bananas.

Here's a sample entry on New York City's Hunt's Point Terminal Market *Fresh Fruits and Vegetables News,* and how it decodes:

BROCCOLI: SLSTGR ctns 14 bchs *CALIF* 6:50 few hias 7.00 occ loas 6.00 *ARIZ* 6.00

Which Means: BROCCOLI: Slightly stronger (prices going up) in cartons of 14 bunches each, from California, for 6.50, a few cartons as high as 7.00 and occasionally some as low as 6.00; cartons from Arizona at 6.00

To translate this information into pricing for each member, take the per container price and divide it by the number of items or pounds in the container. For example, if you choose broccoli from Arizona, it will cost $6.00 for 14 bunches, or $.428 per bunch.

How to Buy from Farmers

Several regions of the country have a large number of farms of many varieties, producing fruits, vegetables, grains, poultry, dairy products, and other foodstuffs. If you live at all close to any of these farms, I recommend strongly that the co-op consider making direct purchases regularly from the farmers, even if the arrangement is only seasonal. Learn what fruits and vegetables are grown locally and when they are in season. (If you are new to the area, ask someone who grew up there.) Seeking out locally grown produce saves both time and money.

Farmers are generally easier to negotiate with; they are generally more knowledgeable about what they're selling, since they themselves grew it; they are generally more honest about quality. Many co-ops have made it a policy to deal with as many farmers as possible because they can buy from the farmers at lower prices, because they support regional economics, because they enjoy organic foods grown without pesticides, herbicides or fungicides, or else because they feel that small family-run farms are endangered by the huge agribusiness conglomerates which squeeze them off their lands and out of their rightful profits.

Whatever your group's reasons for dealing with farmers, remember that farmers operate in four different ways:

1) Farmers may make their crops available for sale at the regular wholesale market, the terminal market, or at a specially designated Farmer's Market.

2) Farmers may open their land for a few hours each week

and allow buyers, including co-op buyers, to drive out and purchase foods.

3) Farmers may take orders by telephone and make deliveries to the co-op's distribution point like any other distributor.

4) Farmers may agree to contract for a certain quantity of certain foods over a period of several months at a set price which the co-op guarantees it will buy.

In most of these arrangements, your dealings with the farmer would be the same as with any other food wholesaler, and not be more complicated or include less of a guarantee. Should the co-op plan to purchase directly from farmers, keep these points in mind:

1) In exchange for sizable savings on foods over even the wholesale market price, in most cases, you may receive fruits and vegetables that are unwashed, unbunched or in mixed sizes in the same container.

2) The cost of the actual bushel basket or crate is an important one, and some farmers prefer to have customers put down a deposit and then return the baskets for a refund, or else to provide their own baskets, boxes, or bags for carting away the purchased produce.

3) Contracting with a farmer may or may not be done in writing. The business arrangement can begin on a small scale and gradually become more substantial as the co-op finds satisfaction in the quality, reliability, and low prices of the produce and as the farmer develops a sense of trust that the co-op will make good on its word. It could start as simply as asking a dairy farmer to deliver 15 dozen eggs each week for the co-op unless otherwise notified of any change the night before delivery day.

4) Some items may not be of the weight or appearance usually found in the supermarket (national chains purchase truckloads of produce from one section of the country and ship it to all their stores). For instance, you may receive fresher, cheaper, naturally grown tomatoes from the local farmer, but they may not be perfectly round or of uniform size or color.

Overall, using farmers as a local natural resource will tend to broaden both the co-op's savings and its sense of community.

How to Buy Other Foods

In exploring sources for all the food categories described below, remember that to obtain these foods, no actual "shopping" is required. Instead, an order is placed to be picked up or delivered. Payment is made in advance or when the items are received, or, rarely, by check after a bill has been sent.

The questions below relate to *every category* and should be asked when researching any supplier, food producer, or wholesaler handling any of the foods discussed in this section.

1) Is a minimum order required, and what is that minimum? Some minimums will be quoted in dollars, others in cases or cartons or pounds.

2) How are orders placed? Can they be phoned in? How long in advance must the order be received?

3) Must orders be paid for in advance? Is a deposit required? Can payment be made by check? Are they authorized to accept food stamps directly?

4) Do they deliver? Under what conditions? Hours and days of the week? What is their delivery charge? Must someone sign for all delivered goods? Is the driver authorized to accept goods being returned, to accept goods that are damaged or of poor quality, or to accept payment in cash?

5) What provisions must be met to return damaged, spoiled, or inferior-quality goods? Can credit be extended on your next purchase, instead of getting a cash refund?

6) How will they keep the co-op informed of all the food items they have for sale, and at what prices? Will they honor previously quoted prices if the price rises in the period between the quote and the purchase?

7) Are they doing business with any other co-ops? Is there any particular representative in their company you should deal with regularly?

All these questions should be considered when dealing with any new wholesale distributor. The special questions that apply to each separate category are listed below. Keep in mind that different types of foods may often be available from a single wholesale distributor. For instance, a butcher may also carry eggs. Or a dairy outlet may also have bacon. Bakeries may be a source of honey, nuts, dried fruits, chocolate chips, or other bakery supplies. If the person you're talking with at a wholesale place happens to mention that they also handle additional items, refer to the questions below that pertain to those items in order to complete the research.

Dairy Outlets Freshness is probably the most pressing requirement for any dairy product. If the co-op cannot locate a local dairy farmer to deal with, then it will have to deal with a dairy wholesale distributor. When investigating such distributors, find the answers to these questions:

1) Exactly what do they deal in, and in what unit amounts? What bulk quantities? (For example, 8-ounce yogurt may come in a 12-container carton, while quart-sized yogurt may only be packed six or eight to a carton.)

2) How fresh are the products they carry? Do they purchase from a farmer or a large producer, or are they selling their own products?

3) If delivered, how long will the items have been on the delivery truck? Is the truck refrigerated?

4) Do they charge less if eggs are delivered in 30-dozen cardboard cartons than if packed separately in one-dozen crates? Would the cost be reduced further if you recycled back to them the cardboard dividers used in the 30-dozen containers?

5) Do their butter and margarine come wrapped in paper? If so, is the paper-wrapped kind less expensive than boxed butter or margarine? Do they carry 5-pound blocks of butter or margarine? Do they carry the institutional-size 60-pound block?

6) Do they offer cottage cheese and yogurt? Do they have plastic and cardboard containers available? Are the cardboard ones cheaper? Is the 8-ounce yogurt available in flavors?

7) What sizes do their cheeses come in? How are they wrapped? Do they handle both domestic and imported cheeses? Will they describe exactly where the different varieties come from, for instance Cheddar and Swiss?

8) Do they handle milk? Can it be delivered fresh the morning it will be distributed? Do they handle half-gallon and gallon sizes? Is the milk available in cardboard cartons for less money than in plastic bottles?

The Butcher Most small co-ops are not able to carry an extensive selection of meats for one basic reason. They do not have the time, the facilities or the skills to turn a large slab of meat into individual portions. Because of this, they will try to locate a meat wholesaler who will sell them meat items that are already portioned, such as unsliced loaves or sticks of luncheon meat, packages of bacon, and canned hams. If you can find a butcher who will make available such portions as a 3-pound package of lamb chops or a one-pound package of ground meat, your co-op might expand its selection of meats.

Whatever the selection, keep these questions in mind when tracking down a meat wholesaler.

1) What do they carry, and in what quantities? Will they make portion packages available to you? What will the portions be wrapped in?

2) Are there any special kinds of meats your group may be glad to hear about? (For instance, grass-fed beef, kosher meats, organic chickens, chemical-free bacon or salami.)

3) How is the meat inspected? Is it local or shipped into the region? Does the weight include the packaging?

4) Will specials available to retail outlets be available also to the co-op?

An area farmer may be willing to supply the co-op with some meats. When consulting farmers about dairy items, ask about meat and poultry items.

The Bakery There are three possible sources of supply for baked goods that the co-op should consider. One is the large, regional wholesale bakery operation, which supplies area supermarkets with sliced, wrapped breads and rolls. The second is the regional representative of any of the national baking chains, which produce breads, rolls, English muffins, desserts, and other baked goods. The third is the local bakery shop. (Actually, a fourth possibility is a member of the co-op who bakes his or her own bread and makes it available for sale to the other members.) All three commercial outlets should be asked the following questions if interested in selling to the co-op:

1) Will the products available for the co-op to purchase be fresh or day-old?

2) Can loaves of bread be sold sliced for the same price as unsliced?

3) Do they carry special products the members might be interested in, such as diet breads, holiday baked goods, bagels, or organic baked goods?

4) How are the baked goods packaged?

Dry Goods/Natural Foods Distributors This dual category is actually far larger than it might seem at first glance. It includes regular dry goods, such as beans of all kinds, flour, rice, lentils, split peas, dried fruits, nuts, noodles, spaghetti, and dried milk. It also includes natural food products such as honey, organic peanut butter, natural jams and jellies and preserves, teas, tamari, wheat germ, preservative-free mayonnaise, and cooking oil. They are combined here simply because the type of operation run by distributors of either group is usually very similar, and in some cases, one distributor may handle both categories of foods.

When contacting a distributor for these items, check on these questions:

1) Is there a recently issued catalogue available that lists their products, the various quantities they come in, and current prices?

2) How are the various items packaged? For instance, are one-pound packages of barley wrapped in plastic or cellophane? Are the bulk quantities of nuts packaged in sacks, bags, or metal containers?

3) How do they certify that the organic items they carry are actually organic?

4) Do they ever knowingly substitute a similar item for one they are out of? For instance, if the co-op has ordered 50 pounds of green split peas, and all they have on delivery day is yellow split peas, would they substitute without telling someone from the co-op in advance? (What does the co-op think of this type of policy, which is likely to happen only in this category of foods?)

5) If they quote a price by telephone on Friday and by the time a shopper goes to pick up the co-op's order the following Thursday the price has risen, will they honor their previously quoted price?

Bulk quantities from dried-goods wholesalers generally fall into a few standard bulk amounts. Bottled or packaged goods, such as peanut butter, dried fruit, teas, pasta, cereals and flours come in multiples of 6 to a carton. These items are nearly always available 12 to a carton, and then sometimes in 6-to-a-carton and 24-to-a-carton sizes also, with price adjustments downward in relation to the increase in the number of packages per carton.

Foods that come loose, such as rice, all kinds of beans,

some cereals, seeds, nuts, flour, and dried fruit, can be bought in 25-pound, 50-pound, and 100-pound sacks. Occasionally, some varieties are available in 75-pound sacks as well.

Liquid items such as juices, maple syrup, cooking oil, and soy sauce, generally come in 8-ounce bottles and in pint, quart, gallon, 5-gallon containers. Some cooking oil may be purchased in 55-gallon drums. Honey comes in one-pound, 5-pound, and 60-pound containers.

Canned and Bottled Goods This group of foods usually is the least likely to be available to small co-ops. The reasons are that supermarkets sell these products at a very low profit margin to attract customers into the store, and distributors are not apt to sell fewer cases than their minimum, which can be in the range of a few hundred cases! The co-op's best source is the regional distributor of canned and bottled foods, the independent producer, or the local ethnic importer. With any of them, ask these questions:

1) What is the estimated shelf life of their items, in the event the co-op wants to buy a quantity too large for immediate sale and plans to store the surplus to sell in a month or two?

2) Do they carry extra large, economy, giant, or other bulk sizes of bottled and canned goods, usually sold only to institutions such as hospitals, schools and camps?

3) How many units to a case?

4) Will they ever, under any circumstances, sell you split cases? (Split cases are part of a full case of an item, and this is an extremely rare practice. It would mean, for instance, that if your order were for fourteen bottles of tomato sauce, and they come twelve to a case, they would open a second case to give you the extra two bottles.) Only ask this question of the distributor who seems unusually willing to make any accommodations to serve the co-op.

Other Considerations on Buying Foods Wholesale

Cash vs. Check In the beginning and until the wholesalers know the co-op very well, all the bills will probably be paid in cash. The exceptions, if any, would be a few suppliers of dried foods, distributors of bottled or canned goods, or any large national company doing business with you through a regional branch office.

A bank account would be necessary if the co-op plans to accept food stamps from members, but receiving that type of authorization requires that the group be an ongoing operation. Setting up a bank account should not be a priority, therefore, and could wait until the food stamp authorization process is under way. (See Food Stamps, page 116)

The co-op may, however, decide to open an account for its own convenience. Once the money system (pages 71–79) has been chosen by the group and put together adequately, it will be much easier to discuss the pros and cons of a checking account for your group. If the decision is yes, keep these points in mind:

1) Double signatures on checks, so no one person can authorize payments.

2) Accessibility of the bank both in hours of the days it's open and in its location in relation to where the money is collected.

3) Availability of a commercial checking account, its advantages and disadvantages.

4) How often statements are issued, and to whom they should be mailed.

5) How long it takes for deposits to be payable.

If the group decides at some future time to open a checking account, refer back to this list before setting it up.

Long-Distance Buying Negotiating with suppliers in remote areas is not the ideal way of purchasing foods and should be considered only if there is no other way to obtain food the co-op wants. If your co-op is too far from a source of supply for dried foods (lentils, beans, etc.) or canned and bottled goods of a special nature, you might think about contacting wholesalers or distributors in another part of the country and having a bulk order shipped to you.

Poll the members to learn if anyone has a friend or relative living near a source of supply. If so, perhaps that person would be willing to do your purchasing and shipping for you. Often, bus lines will ship goods much faster than any other means of transport, sometimes within a matter of hours. In this case someone from the co-op would be needed to meet the bus and claim the parcel.

Before you place an order with a wholesaler, distributor, or anyone, here are a few things to think about:

1) Make certain the packaging is done in a waterproof container. Dried foods will generally not be ruined by temperature changes (sitting in a delivery van in Mississippi for eighteen hours; last on the list of items for delivery in Maine), but moisture will start some seeds (all beans, peas, lentils, etc., are actually seeds) germinating and therefore will eventually begin spoilage.

2) Delivery must be made to an address where someone is available during business hours. If your co-op address is a garage, church basement, or other nonresidence, make sure any foods ordered for shipment are sent where someone can receive them, and sign and pay for them. Get an estimated time of arrival.

3) Find out from your source of supply what quantities the foods will be shipped in. For example, 50 pounds of garbanzos coming in one container will not qualify for the U.S. Post Office's low-rate fourth-class category because it enforces a 40-pound maximum limit. Two 25-pound containers, however, would qualify.

4) The shipping organizations charging low rates will not knowingly accept perishable foods for shipment. And my advice is never to ship any food that may spoil; stick to items like rice, dried beans, etc.

5) Ask the source of supply and the shipper about insurance.

Shipping Charges If you can't find someone in the region of the distributor who will send the shipment out to you by bus, then you'll need to consider one of the usual shipping organizations. Use the following information to learn about their policies and the comparative general range of their costs. Because shipping charges will fluctuate, they should be checked frequently.

During the writing of this book (December 1974–January 1975), the U.S. Post Office offered lower rates than United Parcel Service and R.E.A. Express. The Post Office's fourth-class for parcel post rate, which carries a 40-pound maximum weight limitation and is delivered via rail service, is determined by a combination of weight of the parcel and the distance between the point of origin and destination. They have a "zone" system, which means that goods are charged certain flat rates from one zone, or region, of the country to another, the price depending also on the weight of the package. Any post office will quote rates for you.

The U.S. Post Office quoted an estimate on December 30, 1974, for two 25-pound packages of dried beans leaving Emmaus, Pennsylvania (zip code 18049), and arriving in New York City (zip code 10025) at $2.10.

United Parcel Service carries a 50-pound maximum limit on all packages they handle. They, too, offer a weight-plus-zone schedule of rates. If you wish to receive a quote on some items, you should know the zip codes of their places of origin, their weight, and the addresses to which they'll be delivered. Call the nearest U.P.S. office in your town or city. If there is no office within your regular dialing area, check your telephone directory for the nearest office. Mr. Dan Buckley of the New York City U.P.S. stated that U.P.S. will accept collect calls from individuals wishing information about rates. Also, if by chance you live in an area serviced by an independent telephone company—one that does not belong to the national listing system for Yellow Pages—call, toll-free, the information operator in the nearest town for the phone number of the U.P.S. office there.

U.P.S. quoted an estimate on December 30, 1974 for one 50-pound package of dried beans from Emmaus, Pa. to New York City at $3.28.

R.E.A. Express will ship parcels of any amount and any weight. Its rate structure, however, is far more complex, and varies from town to town, rather than from region to region. R.E.A. will give rate information on the telephone, but will not accept collect calls from individuals.

R.E.A. quoted an estimate on December 30, 1974, for one 50-pound parcel of dried beans from Emmaus, Pennsylvania, to New York City at $24.82.

Systems for Handling the Money

Everything depends on how efficiently the money is handled in the co-op. Members will have to collect money for food, pay money to purchase it, cover additional expenses with money, and turn money into checks for items not paid for in cash.

There are various ways to handle the co-op's money transactions, and the choice, of course, will be up to the members. Some systems may not seem suited to the group, while others may be just right for your co-op's size, membership, and location.

Most co-op veterans advise against building into your system—especially at the outset—an attitude of extending credit when money is due.

Here's a description of the most popular forms of money systems:

The Potluck System

This method is used by the very smallest of groups, five to ten members or households. It may be employed by larger groups, but beyond a certain number of members its simplicity becomes a limitation rather than an asset.

Each household puts in a prearranged amount of money. The shoppers go to market, deduct at the outset any incidental expenses such as gas and tolls, and with the remaining money, purchase the most and the best for the group's money. For example, if five households belong and each puts in $6, the shoppers may, for their $28.20 (assuming gas and tolls cost $1.80), get 50 pounds of potatoes, a carton of 88 oranges, a bushel carton of apples, a bushel basket of endive, 12 heads of cabbage, 5 pounds of roasted peanuts, and 5 bunches of fresh mint.

When the bulk food is delivered to the pickup point, the packing crew divides it all up five ways. Each household would receive for their $6: 10 pounds of potatoes, 17 oranges, about 10 apples, a large head of endive, two or three cabbages, a pound of roasted peanuts, and a bunch of fresh mint.

This is also a simplified system for dividing up the food, since it is easily broken into equal shares. Should a large household be interested in more food, it could pay $12, and get two shares of the total bulk order. Any extras can be divided up however the group wishes.

A flow chart of this system at its basic level looks like this:

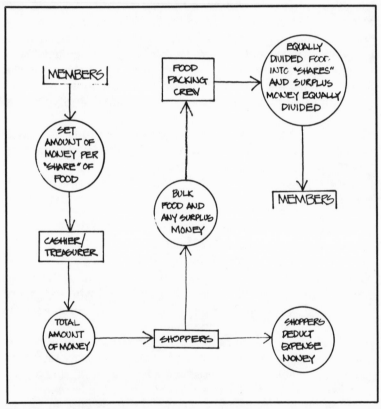

The Potluck System

Here are some considerations your group should discuss if it is interested in this system:

1) The discretion of the shoppers always determines what

you get for your money. Members' tastes should be quite similar. Otherwise, someone may pay for food he or she won't use.

2) Shoppers must have a sense of wholesale amounts, and how they translate into the group's and the individuals' needs. A shopper should keep in mind what the individual portion would be for any items bought in bulk. Some people may not be very pleased to receive 11 pineapples, however cheap they may have been.

3) The money end of the potluck system has only one basic rule—members must pay in advance. Shoppers should never have to put money in for someone else. Incidents have occurred in which a member in a potluck system who indicated an interest in buying a share for a certain week refused both the food and the payment because he didn't like all the choices made by the shoppers. In this situation, the other members are forced to pay for the extra food.

4) Leftover money is returned to each member equally.

5) You might have someone serve as treasurer and have her or him collect the money from each member and then deliver the total amount of money to the shoppers. The remaining members would divide up the food after it has been delivered by the shoppers to a distribution point.

6) Members might indicate certain food preferences or items they definitely do not want when turning in their money, and this information could be passed along from the treasurer to the shoppers.

Preorder/Prepaid Credits System

In this system and the following one, each member fills out an order form, listing or checking off food preferences, before the shopping is done.

Preorder/prepaid order forms include a price for each item, usually determined by the previous week's market price, the current Department of Agriculture produce bulletin, and/or the latest prices quoted by other wholesalers. Once the order form has been completed and the total food quantities are figured out, the amount for the total cost is paid to a cashier or treasurer. When all the orders have been placed and all the money has been collected, a tabulator or collator combines all the individual orders into a master shopping list and makes certain the totals are correct, and that the total money (all the individual order payments) equals the total food prices (the total number of each item multiplied by the cost per item and all totals for all items added together).

The money and master shopping list are then passed along to the shoppers. (The individual order forms are usually then passed along to the packing crew to use in dividing up the bulk order.) Shoppers then purchase the indicated bulk amounts, pick up any phoned-in orders at the wholesalers', and deliver them all to the co-op's distribution center. Any remaining money is put into a revolving fund, and individuals receive credit on their next order for items they paid for and did not receive (due to shortages at the market, drastic rises in price, or occasional inedible food found in the center of a crate which creates an overall shortage). It is possible to return money to each member, but that means you will need (a) to deal with a lot of small change, and (b) to handle this money separately when food is being picked up or ordered at the next meeting.

A flow chart of this system is on the facing page.

Keep these things in mind when planning to set up this system:

1) Attempt to list the most accurate prices possible for each item. Errors will cause problems for the tabulator, the shoppers, the packing crew, and, of course, eventually for every member. Shoppers may find themselves with a master shopping list that calls for 100 pounds of something but may not have enough money to make the purchase, because the estimated price on the order form was too low and not enough money was collected from members. Therefore, they may buy only 75 pounds of that item. Then the packing crew must decide which members will not get the full amount of the food they ordered. Don't fall into the trap of simply using two-week-old prices. Shoppers must realize how important it is to keep an accurate record of how much money they spent for each item, and how important it is to check current prices for foods the group wants to buy the following week. Many variables, such as weather, transportation, holidays, and rumors, influence food prices at the market, and they may jump or drop in a matter of hours.

2) Extending advance credit for someone's full order is extremely unwise. One definite benefit of prepaid orders is that

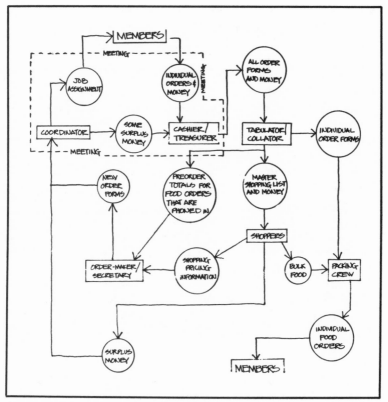

Preorder/Prepaid Credits System

people seldom forget to pick up their food on time, since they've already paid for it.

3) Set a uniform method for filling out the order form. For example, a 2-pound container of cottage cheese should be entered on the order form as "1" (container). If a member has written "2" in the blank space, she would get and be expected to pay for two containers, or 4 pounds of cottage cheese. Remember that the tabulator will check the figures on the sheets, and these errors will eventually show up. Establish policy at the outset to eliminate unnecessary work and food purchases.

4) To aid the tabulator and the packing crew, you might ask members to order foods in whole pound quantities. Anyone wanting 1½ pounds of provolone cheese should find another member willing to buy the extra ½ pound. The combined order should be entered on only one order form and the dividing up of the cheese and the cost of it should be left to the members

involved. (This is a very common practice, and should be encouraged from the beginning. It eliminates all the problems of having to divide per pound costs of items in half, and the tabulator does not have to figure those items out twice.)

5) If you decide on a system in which you pay some or all of your bills by check, or have applied to accept food stamps (see Food Stamps, page 116), then your co-op must have a checking account with a neighborhood bank. You can then deposit money from individual orders, as well as surplus shopping money and Food Stamps, into your account.

Remember that you may not be able to establish credit with some or all of the wholesalers, and therefore should not open an account for the co-op until you are certain the suppliers will accept the group's checks as payment. Never send a shopper to buy or pick up food with a check unless it has been previously confirmed that the check will be accepted as payment.

Also, set a policy at the outset about accepting personal checks from members as payment for food. Many co-ops accept only checks when members leave their order form and payment at a drop-off point. Some accept checks only for the exact amount of the order. Others never accept checks under any circumstances.

6) If members feel there may be a discrepancy about the amount of money claimed as credit, suggest that last week's order form be brought to the ordering meeting or shown to the cashier to verify credit claims. The cashier would then need a record from last week's packing crew as to which foods were not delivered to which households. Here is another example of how trust plays a key part in any co-op system. If members feel that someone is systematically claiming more credit than is due, then encourage a full study of it. If that member is actually doing this, he or she will likely drop out. If not, the group will be more conscious of how important it is for everyone to be honest in a co-op.

Preorder/Pay-on-Delivery System

The same basic pattern is followed in this system as in the preorder/prepaid credits system, with one important difference: no money is collected at the time food is ordered. Instead, the first week a member joins, a food money deposit is collected equal to an approximate order. The shoppers then use one-week-old money to buy the wholesale food. The actual money used to shop this week will be last week's collected money. This means an initial outlay of money must be collected from each member when he or she joins. For instance, if Ambrose and Sue decide to join, they estimate their average weekly order at $12, and deposit that amount. When they fill out the order form, either no prices or guideline prices will be listed next to the items. Their actual bill is figured out after the shopping has been done, based on the cost of the foods paid by the shoppers, and they pay the exact amount they owe when picking up the food. Ambrose and Sue's $12 go into the payment fund, covering their first week's food; the money they pay when they get that food is put into the shopping fund for next week. A new member, therefore, pays twice the first week only, and very little or nothing when leaving. During their final week with the co-op, Ambrose and Sue pay only the difference between their total food bill for that week and their initial $12.

This system might be compared to the one-month security payment a tenant pays when first moving into a rented apartment or house. The payment is kept until the tenant moves out, and can be used to cover the last month's rent or the cost of any damages the tenant may have caused.

A flow chart of this system follows:

Most co-ops serving a dozen or more members use order forms that are printed-up or duplicated set of sheets listing food items available. There are many possible variations in devising the order form; what information is included and how it is used by members all depend on how the group operates. These specifics will be dealt with in detail later on; for now, just keep in mind that the order form serves as a device for members to write down what foods and in what amounts they want. This allows the information to be compiled, or tallied, more readily, and facilitates every step in the co-op's ordering-buying-paying-distributing system.

Order forms used in some operating systems allow members to tabulate the amount of their food co-op bill. At the bottom of these types of order forms are specially drawn lines and spaces to aid in their addition.

In almost every system, order forms are returned to members when they receive their food. This enables them to make a

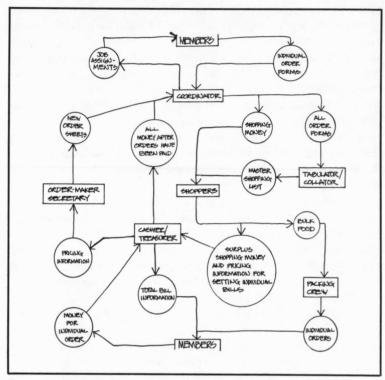

Preorder/Pay-On-Delivery System

final check to be certain that what they got was what they ordered.

If adopted, this system should have the following features:

1) the person acting as cashier/treasurer must be available the day shopping and pickup are done, since that's when money is collected from members. The per pound or per item costs of the food computed by the cashier will be based on the records and receipts kept by the shoppers. Even foods that have been preordered and phoned in will have with them a receipt which the shoppers will get when that food is picked up.

2) There should be no need for credits; as mentioned before, a member, once past the first week, pays only for what is received. The order form may contain guideline prices (or guideline prices may be posted at the ordering meeting or the pickup point, for members' information) to give members an idea of the approximate range their bill will fall into. The ap-

proximate range is based on the most recent pricing information available.

3) Instead of being where the individual order forms are filled out, the coordinator may be stationed at the distribution point to give out job assignments. If that's the case, the new order forms would go from the order-form maker to the tabulator directly, who would then supervise the filling out of each individual's order, check the figures, and keep the completed form.

4) A variation of the system in which each member comes to a central place to fill out an order form (which might be called the fill-it-out system) is one where the orders are telephoned in to someone (the phone-it-in system). In this system, members phone either the tabulator, the coordinator, the order-form maker or—a new position—the order taker. Whoever it is, that person takes each household's order by phone, and passes the order forms along to the tabulator. The usual problem with this system is that there can be disagreement over any mistakes made in recording items. The advantage is the elimination of a trip to a central place to fill out the forms.

5) Another variation, very popular, is to make the new order forms available somewhere convenient to all members. A co-op could use an empty mailbox in the community room of an apartment building to leave the blank forms, or put them in a neat pile near the cash register of the neighborhood dry cleaning store or on a table in the waiting room of the dentist's office. Once members have filled out their forms, they could slip them under the tabulator's door, leave them in the mailbox or put them through a mailslot, making sure the forms are turned in before the prearranged deadline so that the tabulator will have enough time to do all the necessary calculations.

Order forms could also be made available in advance to members in a preorder/prepaid credits system in order to give members an opportunity to fill out their forms after checking their household stock of food.

If the co-op is offering exactly the same items from cycle to cycle, especially in the beginning stage, a large number of standardized order forms could be made available and members could turn in new ones when food is picked up. Be certain a date is written in on top of the form so there's no chance of someone getting an old order form.

Collecting Extra-Expenses Money In All Systems

Beyond the wholesale costs of the foods, other expenses must be considered, even in the most simply run co-ops. The most common additional expenses are:

1) gasoline and oil for the shopping vehicle;

2) tolls, if the shopping trip entails them;

3) small equipment and supplies, such as scales, marking pens, pencils, cheese-cutting knife, waxed paper, etc., that can't be obtained for free;

4) rent, if your group has no other choice (even churches may require a monthly "donation" to use the basement);

5) unexpected small rises in the price of some items. For example, if baby lima beans move up from 29¢ per pound to 30¢ per pound, shoppers would likely still purchase them rather than disappoint members who have ordered them. But that small increased amount of money must come from somewhere, and over time, items that everyone orders will fall into this small-increase category.

Possible ways for raising this money are discussed below. Keep in mind that these systems are generally used for on-going, time-after-time expenses, but could also be used to raise a large amount of money, over a period of weeks, for larger expenses, such as wire snips to open some types of crates bound with wire, or a pocket calculator for the tabulator and shoppers.

1) In the potluck system, each member simply pays a surcharge on the cost of the food, unless, as recommended earlier, the expenses have been deducted from the total money put in. For example, if six households put $5 each into the shopping fund, expense money of $1.80 could be taken off the top, leaving $28.20 to shop for food, instead of $30 (6 × $5 = $30). If not, the $1.80 could be divided by the number of members ($1.80 ÷ 6 = $.30), and the extra $.30 collected when the food is picked up.

2) In the other systems, a tax on each order could be collected. For example, 5 percent could be charged on a household's order of $20, making the total bill $21 ($20 × .05 = $1). Many co-ops feel this is the fairest method of

raising the needed revenue because a person is taxed or assessed according to the amount of food purchased.

In the preorder/prepaid credits system, a line is added at the bottom, below the total, of the order form, for figuring this additional expense, and the money is collected with the order.

The Broadway Local uses this system, and here's what the total lines look like on an average order form:

MONEY SUMMARY

Produce	_____
X-LARGE BROWN EGGS	_____
Meat	_____
Dairy	_____
People's Resources	_____
Grain	_____
Bread	_____
SUB-TOTAL	_____
+ 5%	_____
SUB - TOTAL	_____
Credits	_____
NET CASH	_____

In the preorder/pay-on-delivery system, the tax is figured by the cashier into the total amount owed.

The tax could rise or fall according to the ongoing expenses. An ambitious cashier or bookkeeper or order-form maker could even refigure the tax each time, have it go up to 6 percent or 7 percent, or down to 2 percent or 3 percent. How-

ever, it is wise to have a set percentage which members ca ˌ
expect. It will take a few cycles to determine just what percentage covers these expenses. Be certain members understand
that once the best percentage has been determined, it will remain at that figure.

3) A system called "direct charge" is popular in some
Canadian co-ops. In this system, each household pays only the
cost of the food when it orders or picks up. At the end of each
month, the total dollar amount of accumulated expenses is divided by the number of adults (you could count children as ½),
and each household then must pay this amount, regardless of
how much or how little it has ordered. This system is seen both
as an incentive to have people order as much food as possible
from the co-op and as a lever in eliminating nonparticipating
members or those who do not volunteer for jobs. People not
paying their surcharge are dropped until they pay. New members usually pay a fee equal to an average order.

4) A system that adds a penny or two to the wholesale
price of each item can be used in both preorder/prepaid credit
and preorder/pay-on-delivery systems. This "hidden tax" may
be easier for some members to accept until they recognize that
it actually can be very unfair unless done on a strict percentage
basis. For example, taking apples and cheese, an addition of 1¢
per apple, from 8¢ to 9¢ apiece, is a percentage increase of about
12½ percent; but a 2¢ addition to the price of cheese, from
$1.20 to $1.22 per pound, is a percentage increase of less than 2
percent. Of course, the inequity is even greater if all you buy
are apples and other items similarly jacked up in price in terms
of percentage, and do not ordinarily buy cheese, meats, one-
gallon containers of cooking oil, or other more expensive items.

Whichever system your group uses to collect this needed
money, be certain that you don't begin to collect far more than
you need to balance out the expenses. If you have obtained a
nonprofit organization status, you must not make any profit
beyond your operating costs. Also, extra money may tend to
encourage shoppers and tabulators to become less careful in
their jobs. If extra money accumulates, either designate a use
for it, or eliminate the tax for a week or two until the surplus
has been returned to the average cushion amount your group
needs. If the surplus reappears, reduce your markup propor-
tionally.

Systems for Handling the Distribution of Food

The group will need to devise a system for distributing the bulk order, dividing it up into each household's order; research for such a system must be done carefully. The first time members confront boxes, crates, bushels and bags of produce, grains, meats or whatever else is purchased, after the weary shoppers have deposited them on the floor of the distribution center, they'll be glad an appropriate distribution system to get things rolling has been agreed on.

The four systems described below will more or less accomplish the task of putting your groceries on your own kitchen table. Some work better than others, depending on the group's size and location. Perhaps parts of two or three systems could be combined to suit the needs of the co-op more perfectly. Think about and discuss these systems very closely, because it's the pay-off stage for the co-op. Continuing foul-ups time after time in the distribution step, even more than in other areas, will weaken the co-op considerably, and could eventually cause it to fail.

To Each His/Her Own

The least efficient system, and one I do not recommend, this setup has each person going into the distribution area, order form in hand, and selecting the items one by one that he or she has ordered. For several reasons, this system is an unwise choice. Early arrivals will get all their foods, while those who cannot come until twenty minutes before the end of the allotted time period are stuck with having to accept any shortages that may have occurred. This system also makes it necessary for each member to put in an additional twenty to thirty minutes each ordering cycle, filling out his or her orders personally, and this is something likely to be resented, especially by those who have already done some tedious volunteer job earlier in the day.

Around the Room

In this system, the foods are placed on tables around the perimeter of the room or on a double island in the center of the room. A few members arrive early to do two procedures in advance. They weigh out all items bought by the pound, and package them into one-pound parcels. They also arrange the foods in the sequence in which they should be packed into grocery bags. For example, noncrushable items like carrots, bottled goods, or dried beans might be at the first few stations with the more crushable food closer to the end of the line. Strawberries and peaches, along with eggs, might be last.

As members arrive, they pick up their previously filled-out order form and move from station to station along the tables. Volunteers may aid members in completing their order; remaining to help members might be an additional part of the job of arriving early and weighing out the food into pounds and placing it around the room in sequence. This system is far superior to the first one listed; it moves more speedily. Someone at the end of the line could then tabulate the cost of the order if the co-op is not using the prepaid system. Or else that person could simply perform a spot-check through the bags for any errors.

Teams

Dividing into teams speeds up the work time because each order can be filled out in advance and does not require each member to spend a lengthy period completing his or her own order. This system takes "around the room" another step further, with volunteers completing each order after the pound-weighing has been finished. One member of the team takes the filled-in order sheet, while others locate themselves at various food stations. For example, Peter may take the sheet filled out by the Wilson household. He would select the appropriate number of oranges, pears, bunches of celery, bottles of honey, and other items purchased by the piece. He would also

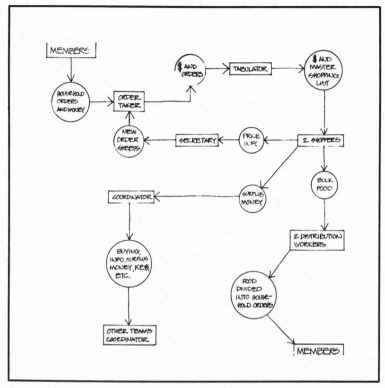

An example of the Teams System approach to Handling the Work

ask "weighers" to measure out the 5 pounds of turnips, the 8 pounds of kidney beans, and the 3 pounds of Cheddar cheese also listed for the Wilsons while he selects the items purchased by the piece, and he would then collect everything into one grocery bag. He would finally tape their order form to the filled grocery bag, ready for them to pick up. This method can be employed by one "team," consisting of someone selecting the counted-out items and one or two weighers, or two "teams" who divide the order forms in half.

Category Order Lists

My personal favorite, this system is the one used on my block, because we've found it to work the best. Back during the tabulating stage, large sheets are used to determine the total amount of each food item collectively ordered by the co-op. The items listed are entered across the top and the household names down the side.

COLLATION/BREAKDOWN SHEET BLOC: ITEMS→ WEEK: PEOPLE↓		ONIONS	POTATOES	APPLES	CABBAGE	NUMBERS	CARROTS	ORANGES	KALE	TURNIPS	NUMBERS	MUSHROOMS	
McANDREW	1	1	10	12	2	1	6	25	2	2	1	2	
JAMES	2	8	10	8	2	2	3	1.5	2	2	2	1	
KOHLI	3	5	6	4	1	3	3	6	1	2	3	1	
MASTRI	4	10	5	10	1	4	.3	1.2	1		4	1	
LEVIN	5	2	8	2		5	2	.5		1	5	1	
CHALLMAN	6	5	10	10	1	6	3	1.5	1	1	6	2	
CHU	7	5	6	8	1	7	2.	6		1	7	1	
PRICE	8	6	10	10	1	8	5	15	1	1	8	2	
SANCHEZ	9	10	2	10	2	9	4	20	2	2	9	1	
CZUBAY	10	3	10	10	1	10	2	5	1	1	10	2	
LEE	11	4	10	15	2	11	.5	10	2	2	11	2	
VESCIA	12	3	10	15	1	12	3	11	1	1	12	1	
	13					13					13		
	14					14					14		
TOTALS	15	62	97	114	15	15	41	145	14	16	15	17	
	16					16					16		
	17					17					17		
	18					18					18		
	19					19					19		
	20					20					20		

Once the form has served its primary purpose and the totals are tabulated, the form can be used, in reverse, for distribution, since it lists on one sheet the households and their complete orders. Numbers down the side of the form, one to a household, are transferred, written large and bold, on the appropriate original order form for each household. They can be written on grocery bags, but writing them on the order forms, which are then attached to the bags, works out better. The tabulating form is then cut into strips, with a few food items contained on each strip.

What each strip contains is a few categories of foods, the numbers of the household orders, and at the bottom, the total co-op order of that item. (When drawing up or printing your tabulating form, remember to incorporate and repeat the number sequence all across the form.)

In this system, one person can do *all* the oranges, *all* the cheeses, *all* the Brussels sprouts. If there's a shortage, the supply can be apportioned fairly among all the orders, because one person will be dealing with the entire distribution of that item. Also, the entire operation runs very smoothly; because it's not necessary for each bagger to deal with every item, each person has fewer food stations to visit.

Considerations and Refinements

For all these systems, except the potluck system, the following are a few points to consider, a few refinements to add, if you wish to do so.

CONSIDER:

1) how important it is just where the different foods are unloaded when they arrive at the group's distribution point. If you're using "around the room" the heavier noncrushable items should be unloaded near a member's first stop around the room so that the heavy food is at the bottom of the bag.

2) the benefits of knowing beforehand exactly which items may contain shortages because of a lack of availability or an increase in price.

3) that you're at all times dealing with foods: don't treat stacking it, unloading it, weighing it, or handling it as you

would books, laundry, or tools. You're working with it to get the best for less money, and eventually, to eat it.

SOME REFINEMENTS:

1) Post a sheet that says "Nobody Got": and list the food the entire co-op will not get that day.

2) Post a sheet that says "Shortages": and ask each volunteer bagger to list these shortages so members can spot at a glance what's missing from their orders. Entry on this sheet should include item, name of household shorted, and amount shorted, such as "Pitted Prunes, DelVayo, 4 lbs. short."

3) Post a sheet that says "Surplus" and list what's for sale.

4) Use the boxes, cartons, and crates that foods come in from the terminal market for additional packing of household orders.

5) If you must measure out a pound of something like lentils or split peas (spillable stuff), put your baby scale inside a carton or box to catch any possible spills. If you have hanging scales, place newspaper or a large carton under the scale for the same reason.

6) Always keep a supply of pencils or marking pens at the distribution center for notes to members and for noting shortages.

7) Have some device for letting members know if they've been shorted, especially the weighed items. Not many people have the time, the scales, or the inclination to weigh their orders once they get them home.

8) If volunteer power permits, ask one person to serve as a clearinghouse, for incorrect distribution of foods. For example, if Eric has received an extra dozen eggs, he calls Lori and tells her. Later, David calls Lori, who is serving as clearinghouse, and tells her he is short one dozen eggs. Lori matches them up. This is a perfect volunteer job for someone who cannot handle physical labor, or has a schedule that permits doing co-op work at night only, or only at home.

Finally, here's the checklist procedure for distribution, which we call breakdown on my block. It's printed on a large white piece of cardboard, and anyone new to the task must read it thoroughly before beginning to work.

—Place bags evenly around lobby. Any order of about $8 should receive a second bag, marked with appropriate number *now*. Magic markers are in scales box. Put waxed paper down where cheese will be cut, next to one scale. Place knife there.

Sign up breakdown people as they arrive on back of this sheet. Tape up "Nobody Got" and "Shortages" sheets to wall in prominent place, accessible to breakdown people. Food should be divided among scales and center wall areas. See that weighed items, like some grain items, onions, potatoes, etc., are unloaded near scales.

—Half the breakdown crew should be working on counted items, half on weighed items at all times. One person should begin crating eggs at once. *Be sure* you know which items were bought by the pound, and which ones by the piece. Check an order form if you're not sure.

—Master sheet for 107th Street, the total block's order, will be delivered with food. It lists shortages.

—Begin with solid, hard foods like bottled goods, potatoes, carrots, etc.—nonbruisable, noncrushables. Pack at bottom of bags. If family has 2 bags, pack solid foods at bottom of *both* bags.

—Proceed to medium-consistency foods like hard pears, breads, asparagus. Check small bags for holes.

—Do *not* pack wet items, however hard, at very bottom. Meats, broccoli, etc. will leak through and cause *broken bags!!*

—Use the breakdown strips of paper found in scales box. When an item's been distributed, cross off the word at the top of the list. Indicate on "Shortages" sheet taped to wall which bags are short, and the amount they have been shorted. Before you begin distributing, check the total at bottom of paper strip against actual amount delivered. Spread any shortage among entire group as equitably as possible, *not* only among high-numbered orders or people you know the least well. If 25 pounds of string beans were ordered, the delivery was 2 pounds short, and there were two families that ordered 2 pounds apiece and one family that ordered 21 pounds, short only the large order. If, however, there were 7 one-pound orders and 2 nine-pound orders, the nine-pound orders would be cut.

—Wrap *all* cheeses before distributing them. Cut cheese *only* on waxed paper surface. Use waxed peper to wrap. If none is left, get some at closest store, keep the receipt, and show at next meeting for credit.

—Designate 1 large box for garbage. As other boxes are emptied, use them for individual food orders. Check bottoms. Return all breakdown strips to scales box, along with master sheet. Put these, tape, pencils, knife, etc., in manila envelope.

Don't let anyone come in and ask to pack his own food: too much disruption and unfair to others.

—Treat all foods and all packages as though they were your own.

Systems for Handling the Work

Work—whether you call it volunteer jobs, individual tasks, or helping out—is what keeps a co-op running. How your group handles the work in its operation will determine how well the co-op is serving its membership.

Once you have researched and chosen the kinds of money and distribution systems that fit best your size of co-op and its members, then you can decide on how the people are to be matched to the jobs in those systems. The primary reason for leaving job assignments to the last is that the work system you choose will be affected somewhat by the external factors (sources of supply, their location, days and hours they're open, etc.) built into the money and distribution systems and these are usually beyond your control.

Most work systems include a coordinator, cashier or treasurer, a tabulator, shoppers, a packing crew, and an order-form maker. If any of these terms are new to you, check them in the Glossary.

How often people do these jobs, whether they do them regularly or rotate them, and how each job is connected to the other jobs in the co-op are all detailed in the following pages.

The Everybody-Works-Every-Time System

My favorite, this system operates on one simple rule: If you get food from the co-op this time, you work for the co-op this time.

If many, many people order foods, then the jobs are divided in half, so that each person works half the time. For instance, if it takes about ten hours of work to run things and twenty people order food, each job is divided up so that it takes each person about half an hour.

Some things to remember if you plan to use this system:

1) Everyone must be willing to comply with this system. That means not only agreeing to do something each time, but also being willing to switch or shuffle jobs with someone else who may have a more rigid schedule than you do.

2) A coordinator is vital. Someone must take the responsibility of seeing to it that every job is filled and that every person contributes. This takes both perseverance and a familiarity with each person's usual available hours, personal skills, past experience, and favorite jobs.

3) There must be various ways in which the jobs can be subdivided or combined. For example, the more orders there are in a given week, the greater will be the amount of work needed to divide up the bulk order into those individual orders; light weeks may require only one or two persons on the packing crew, while heavy weeks might demand four to six people to do such work.

4) The group must learn how the whole co-op works. Some weeks, a member may only be able to put in time at a certain hour, and if only one job can be executed at that time, he or she must be willing to do it. This makes for a stronger co-op, since it's less likely for the co-op to foul up or fall apart during a week or two when a few usually key people are not present.

My block of the Broadway Local uses this system, and here are a few examples of how jobs have been sub-divided.

a) One volunteer job used to be collecting the money and checking the arithmetic on individual order forms at the weekly co-op meeting. Now two people do these jobs, one checking arithmetic only, the other making change after the arithmetic has been checked. The cashier/change-maker also writes the name and telephone number of the person acting as clearinghouse this week at the bottom of every order form. A new job was added to this stage. Each week someone is responsible to bring $8 worth of small change to the meeting so that people won't have to wait until the correct change is available. This change-bringer must arrive on time; he or she deducts $8 from this week's order at the cashier's station to cover the money already put in.

b) Our block used to require that someone waited with

the bags of food between 5 P.M. and 6:15 P.M. each Friday to insure that no food was stolen or taken by mistake; that person would also clean up. Now those jobs, on large ordering weeks, are split. The clean-up person can finish his or her job in 25 minutes. And the waiting person can read, crochet, or study during the 75-minute shift without having to worry about extra little things to do.

c) The distribution coordinator used to arrive about 20 minutes early in the apartment-house lobby which is our distribution center and put out the numbered bags, set up the scales, tape up the information sheets, and supervise (and sometimes help with) the unloading of the foods. Now a separate person arrives early, does all these operations and remains until the distribution coordinator arrives. The coordinator no longer needs to spend an extra half-hour preparing for the work of bagging the food.

The Regular and Rotating Jobs System

This system could also use a coordinator to insure that all jobs will be done. Similar to the everybody-works-every-time system, this one includes the regular volunteering of certain people for certain jobs. These members may either be very skilled in a particular area (a bank teller would want to be treasurer) or have a very rigid schedule (a 3-to-11 factory worker who can only work for the co-op during morning hours).

How the work done by the regular volunteers fits together with that of the rotating members who volunteer for or are assigned the remaining jobs depends on group decisions.

The things to keep in mind if your group selects this system:

1) The main precaution should be that no single person become an irreplaceable cog of the co-op wheel of procedure. If that happens, the co-op does not operate when that person is not around.

2) You might place a maximum period of time on each regular job, and allow someone to do that task week after week for, perhaps, three or four months.

3) This system does not assume that each member does a job each week. Therefore, people doing regular, complicated

jobs, such as tabulating or shopping, often work for a stretch, then have no responsibilities for a stretch. The master shopper may buy food for three months, and not be expected to do any work for the next three months.

4) If you alternate the regular jobs, be certain a complete set of new people do not move into key jobs all in the same week. To avoid this, stagger the change-over times. For example, if your co-op decides to have a regular coordinator, two regular shoppers, and a regular tabulator but to rotate the other jobs, and you also decide to switch people in the regular jobs every four months, try switching coordinators in August, replacing one shopper in September, changing tabulators in October, and replacing the second shopper in November. This results in a continuous, smooth transition.

The Work-Credits System

In this system, each task or job is assigned a certain value: for example, serving as overall coordinator may be worth 3 points, while sweeping up after distribution may be worth 1 point. A member may also be expected to collect 5 points per month, using any combination of jobs, over any length of time.

If you discuss this system, then consider:

1) How are the credits recorded and by whom? What leeway will be allowed for unexpected changes of plans? Will points be deducted when that happens?

2) Over what length of time may a member store up points? Can someone work furiously during the three summer months, then take the next six months off from volunteering while still getting food?

3) What happens when a job or two has no volunteers, yet everyone has fulfilled the credit requirements for the month?

4) What will determine the credit value of jobs: time spent, skill required, or a combination of both?

5) What provisions will be made for someone who only gets food every other time or every third time it's available—a real possibility with single people?

Work-credits is actually my least favorite system, mainly because it has the potential to deteriorate into some petty goings-on. A variation of this system is assigning an hours quota per month to each adult or each household in the co-op.

For example, each household may be responsible for 3 hours' worth of work per month, or each adult may be required to spend 2 hours per month on co-op jobs. The same considerations applying to the work-credits system applies to this variation of it.

The Teams System

This system is possible for co-ops of sixteen or more. Basically, the group divides into two or three smaller groups, and each subgroup, or team, is capable of running the entire co-op from start to finish. For example, a group of sixteen divides into an "even team" and an "odd team." The even team does all the work during the even-numbered months (February is the second month, April is the fourth month, etc.) and the odd team takes over during the odd-numbered months (January, March, etc.).

The eight members of each team, responsible for doing all the work for the total membership of sixteen, would be comprised of two shoppers, one order-taker, one tabulator, one secretary, two distribution workers, and an overall coordinator. The secretary would make out a set of new order forms based on last week's prices and price research he or she has done. The order-taker would collect filled-in order forms and money; the tabulator would tabulate the money and the orders for all sixteen members, phone in any pre-order items (such as cheese or dried foods), and pass on the master shopping list, along with the money, to the shoppers. The shoppers would purchase, pick up, and deliver the food to the distribution center, and record pricing information. The distribution workers would divide the food into each household's order, and wait until all food has been picked up by the members. The coordinator makes certain every step takes place and on time, assists when and where necessary, and passes along all needed facts and materials to the other team's coordinator when the switch occurs.

The Hire-the-Broker System

Some large co-ops—rarely those with memberships smaller than twenty-five or thirty—decide early on to hire one person to fulfill one of the key positions at all times. This person may work only eight or ten hours each week, and receive a part-time salary. The hired post is usually that of the food buyer (broker) or at times a bookkeeper/treasurer/coordinator. A person is hired to strengthen the co-op's weak spot and only after every other alternative has been explored. Paid buyers or brokers often work for more than one co-op. I strongly advise against this system being considered seriously at the start, but it should be mentioned here in case any of the members have heard of it and thought it might apply.

To hire someone, a co-op must be convinced that it can absorb the additional regular financial burden of that person's salary, and also be convinced that it wants to turn over that set of decisions to the same person week after week.

In any hire-a-broker system, all the other jobs remain volunteer and may be filled in by any of the previously presented methods. Be certain that each member knows the extent of each job, and knows where the hired person's responsibilities begin and end. Often, people assume that anyone salaried, even part-time, should be free and willing to fill in for volunteers. This is just not the case, and the idea should be dispelled at the outset.

Points to consider if the co-op feels it may want to hire someone at some future time to buy its food:

1) Engaging the services of a food broker involves checking out the broker's reputation with others who use his or her services, determining the minimum order the broker will handle, negotiating delivery services, affixing accountability for wrong and/or poor-quality foods, and deciding whether the co-op or the broker chooses which foods will be offered for sale to members.

2) Contracts to guarantee your broker's services whenever your co-op requires them should then be discussed. Remember that a contract implies obligations in both directions.

3) Many brokers fix at least part of their fee on the amount of food they handle. Fox example, a broker may charge your co-op a flat rate of $10 per shopping trip plus an additional 10¢ per case or carton of food purchased.

4) Liability of the broker for the shopping vehicle must be discussed if the broker is using the co-op's or a member's truck, van, or station wagon.

Food brokers can be found listed in the Yellow Pages, through other co-ops in your region, or through the closest co-op warehouse; you can also find them sometimes at the wholesale terminal market doing their job. And it can be a full-time job for professional brokers, so always keep that in mind.

If the group wishes to hire someone from the community or the co-op itself, the same considerations concerning an outside broker should also apply, because that person will still be doing a vital job and will still be treated differently from the other members.

The practice of hiring someone as a financial/work overseer is less common. In this variation, that person takes care of all money transactions, fixes prices, and delegates volunteer job assignments to members.

A few points to consider when hiring someone as a financial/work co-ordinator:

1) What past experience has the person had? It takes more than skill with numbers to run this phase of a co-op; a knowledge of foods, wholesale pricing, bulk amounts, and a keen awareness of the schedules, abilities, temperaments, and shortcomings of the members are all equally important.

2) This must be a thoroughly trustworthy person. All money decisions will emanate from this position, and there must be no question about his or her integrity, honor, motives, or intentions.

3) Contracts, or at least mutually concluded lists of responsibilities, should be built into the relationship.

4) If the co-op decides to hire someone to do both the buying and the financial/work management, everything listed here, including salary, should be given twice as much thought.

Hiring someone is one prime decision that may spell disaster for a co-op, because, ironically, a group looking out to save money may wind up spending far more than it wished to, in order to afford that hired person. I personally do not recommend hiring someone until the group is so large that there seems to be no other way to pull things together. The Broadway Local serves nearly four hundred families, and no one gets paid a dime, so it is indeed possible for even a large co-op to run on volunteer power.

The problem of raising the money to pay the salary of any hired worker is included in the discussion of collecting money for other expenses besides the cost of food, at the end of the "Handling the Money" section.

Part III: Setting Up Your Co-op

The Second General Meeting

The group now turns its research into action because the second general meeting really marks the end of the initial research stage. From here on, members are part of an ongoing food co-op organization.

Decisions must be made at this meeting, and as at the first one, they should be made by every individual or a representative from every household planning to use the food co-op. Follow the same procedure as with the first general meeting for setting the time and place. Or you might consider having it at or near the space to be used for packing or picking up of the food.

By this time all primary research should have been done. Here's a quick checklist:

1) Members have been located and have committed themselves to building a food co-op. They are fairly well known to each other, have common food tastes and belong to a similar economic level.

2) Research on what foods the group would like to buy wholesale has been done. Sources for these foods have been investigated.

3) The various kinds of money systems, food distribution systems, and work systems are understood by the members well enough to discuss them.

4) The distribution center's location has been discussed. Possible vehicles for doing the shopping have been considered. Meeting places, when necessary, have also been considered.

5) Specific skills, equipment, and information held by individuals have been offered for use by the group.

6) Everyone understands the crucial importance of trust, good record-keeping, sound working patterns, and cooperation to the co-op's life and death.

Once these steps have been completed, the members can forge their own special system. Decisions on the following should then be made at the second general meeting:

1) After reviewing which foods are available from which sources of supply, the group must decide which foods to begin purchasing. The group should know the bulk amounts (such as number of quarts to a case, or number of bunches to a carton) these foods are sold in, so that they can plan how often certain items will be ordered. For example, items like onions and potatoes can be stored in a kitchen drawer, in a wire basket, or in a string bag for weeks, and are also sold in 50-pound bags; Members could take advantage of a very low per-pound price (even lower in a 100-pound-bag size), order a few weeks' supply, and only list these items every other time the group orders.

2) A distribution center where the group's food is packed into household orders and picked up must be selected. It should contain all the suggested features mentioned on page 33. If keys are needed, arrange for copies to be made and distributed to members who will need them.

3) A shopping vehicle, or several which would rotate, must be agreed upon. The group's responsibility toward it and access to it must be discussed and generally understood.

4) A regular mailing address for catalogues, price lists, bank statements, Department of Agriculture market news publications and other materials must be chosen. If any foods are to be delivered, the location and responsibilities of the person who lives there must be set.

5) The length of time between shopping—weekly, every other week, monthly—must be determined.

6) Decide whether regular weekly or monthly meetings are to be held, and if not, how special meetings can be covered.

7) A complete system for collecting money, shopping, packing the food and allocating the volunteer work must be worked out after examining the systems and examples pre-

sented. Various combinations are possible and some of them are discussed further in this section.

8) If a once-only membership fee has been adopted, it should be collected at this meeting. Keep a record of who has paid. If it is to be refundable, make out receipts.

9) A method of collecting money for initial expenses must be worked out. If it is a straight fee to be levied at the outset, collect it now.

10) The method of collecting money for extra expenses that occur week to week must be decided on.

11) A list of all members, including their addresses and various day and night telephone numbers, should be compiled. Copies should be made and passed out to every member.

After these decisions have been made, assemble a flow chart showing how your co-op's system will operate during a typical buying period. Do this at the meeting so each member can see exactly how the co-op will run, and what each job entails.

The flow chart should spark some additional discussion on exactly what each volunteer job includes, and where one person's job ends and another's job begins. One small co-op in Pennsylvania, which uses the preorder/prepaid credits system for its money, adopted a general rule that it is always the responsibility of a person to deliver whatever materials are involved in their job to the next person in the line of operation. For example, the order-form maker must deliver the new forms to the coordinator, and the tabulator must deliver the money and the master shopping list to the shoppers. That way, there's no confusion about where responsibility lies and little chance of someone both picking up and delivering materials.

End the meeting with an agreement on what day the group will place its first order. Once the schedule has been set, stick to it. Members will have a lot to learn and a lot to remember; imposing a fluid, uncertain schedule on them will only cause problems and discontent.

Starting Small

The "small" here refers to two things, both of which are important. The first is, of course, the size of your group. You now realize how easy it is to create a sophisticated, responsive, money-saving, stable food co-op with as few as eight people, and that you can have a system tailored to your members that provides them with a healthy selection of foods.

The second "small" refers to the initial scope of your buying. In the early period, I advise keeping the foods ordered at one time to no more than ten or twelve items. This increases the probability of garnering a wholesale quantity for each item, and also makes the learning of the whole co-op process far less complicated for everyone. In the beginning, members must learn how to put theory (your group's agreed-upon money/buying/work system) into actual practice (actually receiving food and paying money). Once this process is learned, new items can be added with little complication.

So for the first few ordering times, list only a small number of items and use one or two sources of supply only. You'll be surprised at how quickly members acquire a feel for the whole operation. Until that time, keep it simple.

Mixing and Matching Different Parts of Systems In choosing your own special system, keep in mind that the group is composed of individuals, and that the group must attempt to tailor its system to the schedules, skills, and abilities of these individuals. Conversely, the individual members will find that a small food co-op by its very nature, will create some changes in their lives.

All the systems presented in earlier sections of the book are made up of parts. If your group can fit together a work/buying/money pattern from the systems presented, then you should begin matching people to the tasks right now.

Suppose, though, your group likes a particular system, but one aspect of it just does not coincide with the group's activities. The solution? Alter the system to fit the people.

For example, suppose the preorder/prepaid credits system for money makes sense for your group, and you'd all like to use the regular and rotating jobs system to handle the work and would divide up the food using the category lists. Problem: you can't get together on the same night more often than once a month, yet you'd like to order food weekly. Solution: make the order forms available earlier for pickup at a convenient place for a two day-and-night period. Let the person who is responsible for collecting and accepting forms (people could drop by his or her home) serve also as coordinator and then jobs could be signed up when forms are dropped off. Any week-to-week news could be printed on or typed on the order form, or notes could be put with people's food if you need to tell everyone something about that week's shopping. Make this multifaceted collector/coordinator job a regular one for perhaps two months, then let that person volunteer for something that would take far less time and energy for a while.

Or suppose, for example, your group finds the preorder/pay-on-delivery system attractive, chooses to employ the everybody-works-every-time system for work, and likes the around-the-room method of dividing up the food. Problem: the group feels the cashier should not shoulder the responsibility of carrying around large sums of money, because you plan to use a church basement for the food pickup point and the cashier would have to walk home eight or nine blocks after dark. Solution: open a bank account and accept only personal checks as payment when food is picked up, and only for the exact amount owed. Checks could be deposited that same night through a special night-deposit window, and a check could be cashed for the following week's shopping.

Or suppose you plan to use preorder/prepaid credits, along with the everybody-works-every-time for work assignments, and the teams approach to dividing up the food. Problem: your group likes that one adventuresome aspect of the potluck system, in which a smart shopper can take advantage of an unexpected bargain. Solution: give each member the option of putting in an additional sum, perhaps 50¢, and then let the shoppers loose in the market with this money. The only restrictions are that it not be something already on the list (or almost like it), and that it be something members could enjoy without a major effort to cook it. Some co-ops doing this call it their "mystery item."

Whatever the minor problem is in any system the group wants to use, it is adjustable. Simply scan the other systems and select out one part that will accomplish the same purpose as the part in question.

Regular Meetings The decision may be made to have the order forms available and permit members to fill them out at home and return them. If so, be certain you have agreed on some way a general meeting can be convened when necessary. It's safe to assume that some problems or points of confusion may emerge that only a membership meeting can straighten out.

Regular meetings are my recommendation, even if they're as infrequent as one each month, and should be decided on at the second general meeting. Get into the habit of expecting a free exchange of ideas so that everyone understands and is involved in the running of things, amd also so no one feels a few "leaders" are in charge of everything (a dangerous attitude to develop in co-ops of any size).

Members can be notified of emergency meetings, or special meetings called outside of the regular schedule, through the food distribution system: notes or notices can be placed in each member's food bag or a notice can be placed on the order form; if your co-op has a telephone order-taker, he or she could inform each person.

For any meeting, prepare an agenda of topics to be covered and stick to it. Read the agenda aloud at the start and ask for additions to it. Keep minutes at all meetings.

Collecting Initial Capital To begin, money must be collected before the first order is placed. One-time-only membership fees are almost universal in food co-ops, ranging from 50¢ to $20, either person or per household, and may be regarded as refundable, nonrefundable, or transferable (you can pass on your membership to your roommate or the person who sublets your apartment if you're away for the summer).

Check back in the research section to determine what equipment and supplies you can get free. Then make a list of what you must buy to determine how much initial capital for equipment and supplies is required.

Discuss at the second general meeting who is to be responsible if something gets lost or broken. You may want to put someone in charge of keeping track of things with personal responsibility for replacing lost things, and to have the group pay to replace something that breaks. Or the group may feel it is better to take replacement costs out of everyone's pocket, whatever the cause of the loss.

Defining Clearly All Jobs and Responsibilities Making sure that everyone knows what his or her job is may not be as simple as it sounds. Once certain details have accumulated with each job, it's best to record what these details are, so all members will have a clear idea of what is going on.

After a few shopping cycles, have members write a one-paragraph description of the various jobs co-op members volunteer for. Combine the information into one long paragraph for each job. (Asking more than one peron to write a description of each job insures a wider perspective and a clearer explanation.) Then have all the members read this expanded version. If everyone agrees, mimeograph or duplicate these descriptions and hand them out to everyone. This reduces even further the chance that some small but important step will not get done because someone did not realize it was part of the job he or she volunteered to do.

Be certain the job descriptions include the day and hour by when each job must be completed. Explain what the alternatives are in any emergencies, such as if the shopping vehicle breaks down the night before shopping, or if the basement used for bagging the food has flooded during a heavy rainstorm. These emergency alternate plans should be agreed upon by the membership.

Designing Your Own Order Forms

In some co-op operations, the same type of blank order form is used time after time, with the specifics filled in each shopping cycle. In others, new order forms are prepared each time, with new prices listed or new choices presented. Order forms must do several jobs. Some of the functions an order form should perform are the following:

1) list member's name, address, telephone number, and apartment number;

2) list a date, either the ordering date or the delivery date, which is very important, because a new order filled out on an old order form is of no use;

3) list foods available, including a full identification (juice oranges or navel oranges; red delicious apples or Granny Smith apples; roasted peanuts or unroasted peanuts, shelled or unshelled); also, what quantities they will be divided into and sold by (per pound, per unit, in a 3-pound package, in a 10-ounce container);

4) list pickup date if not a weekly cycle, and pickup point if not a regular location;

5) list prices of foods, and figure out the per item cost—for example, when listing a 3-pound package of veal at $1.20 per pound, show both the per pound cost *and* the total cost, such as $1.20 per pound × 3 = $3.60 per package (prices should be exact if preorder/prepaid credits system, approximate or guideline if preorder/pay-on-delivery system);

6) Include above the totals line any appropriate lines for figuring taxes or surcharges, if any, and for subtracting credits, if any;

7) list the name and phone number of the current coordinator;

8) report any policy changes or procedure alterations;

9) state the drop-off location and deadline for the other order forms, as well as any other rules, if your system includes an order-form drop-off instead of an in-person completion of the order forms;

10) allow space for messages or recipes.

Some co-ops do not have access to duplicating equipment. In that case, they prepare a large number of blank order forms and the order-form maker fills in each by hand each time, writing down the items and amounts; or else the members do this themselves when ordering, using a prepared master copy as a guide.

If you must adopt this system, remember that because the tabulator works from these sheets, it would be wise to insist that every item be written in, even if is not ordered. This makes the task of reading down a column of items and numbers much easier.

Some variations on order forms you might consider include:

1) using different colored paper each week, to reduce further the chances of someone filling out an order on an old form;

2) printing recipes for foods the group will be getting;

3) adding a "preference list" to determine the degree of interest in items not previously ordered by obtaining a sampling of opinion and to learn whether they should be listed for purchase at some future time;

4) writing on the bottom of the order form the name and telephone number of someone who has volunteered to serve as

a clearinghouse, matching up stray or extra foods with rightful owners;

5) passing along information on other food events, such as a $2-per-bushel apple-picking day at a nearby orchard, or a free nutrition workshop at the local college.

Put some serious thought into the design of your order form. It touches every single step in the co-op's overall system; if not planned out carefully, it could result in enthusiasm-draining delays or costly mistakes, either of which could spell disaster for the group.

The following order forms from various food co-ops will give you an idea of the styles and formats used. Your group can copy any one of them, or design and assemble its own, using elements from several forms.

Name _____ Address _____ 2/17/75

Tele _____ Bloc _____ Apt _____

Statistics sheets must be turned in to the Master Collator, Tuesday Nite, together
with your bloc's master order. List number of households ordering each item and
total number of households ordering this week. Results will appear in co-op newsletter.(Master collator, mail to Howard Fink, 202 W. 107 St. Apt 4W, NY NY 10025.

Item	Price			
Mushrooms	.85 Lb.			
Onions (medium)	.08 Lb.			
Peppers (medium)	.40 Lb.			
Spinach	.30 Lb.			
Sweet Potatoes	.15 Lb.			
Tomatoes	.40 Lb.			
Bananas	.15 Lb.			
Cabbage	.27 Hd.			
Carrots (small-medium) cello	.21 Pk.			
Celery	.30 Bu.			
Cucumbers	.17 Ea.			
Eggplant	.33 Hd.			
Scallions	.15 Bu.			
Leeks	.65 Bu.			
Romaine Lettuce	.35 Hd.			
Red Delicious Apples	.08 Ea.			
Avocadoes	.45 Ea.			
Juice Oranges	.05 Ea.			
Navel Oranges	.08 Ea.			
Bosc Pears	.09 Ea.			
Lemons	.08 Ea.			
			TOTAL	

X-LARGE brown eggs are produced in Maine and shipped FRESH to NY each week. LARGE
size eggs are listed in the dairy area and are, presumably, cold storage, supermarket type eggs. We will shortly decide on a more specific type of policy in re-
spect to eggs. Your feedback for Wednesday meetings is therefore required.

Item	Price			
X-LARGE BROWN EGGS Doz.	.73		←TOTAL ←	

Item	Price			
Whole Chicken 3 1/2 Lb	2.24		See other side for 20 min-	
Ground Chuck 2 Lb.	2.52		ute chicken liver recipe.	
1 Lb. Chicken Livers	.91		If you don't like chicken	
1 Lb. Kosher Hot Dogs	1.55		livers, then this recipe is	
Cuduhy Bacon Lb.	1.34		for you. It is worth trying	
Cross Rib Roast 3 Lb.	4.44		anyway; this is a new taste	
		MEAT TOTAL		

Item	Price			
Sweet Butter (AA) Lb.	.91			
Margerine (veg.) Lb.	.60			
Cottage Cheese (Friendship) Lb.	.72			
Muenster Cheese Lb.	1.20			
Cheddar (Vermont) Lb.	1.65			
LARGE-Size Eggs Doz.	.62		(SEE ABOVE NOTE, PLEASE)	
			TOTAL	

People's Resources

Item	Price			
Grape Juice 24 Oz. .49 .49 .49				
Prince Spaghetti Sauce 23 Oz.	.54		(meatless)	
Black Eye Peas 1 Lb.	.26			
Red Kidney Beans 1 Lb.	.42			
American Cheese 1 Lb. IN SLICES	1.00			
			TOTAL	

At least one person in eac bloc should be receiving the FRES HUNT'S POINT BULLETIN.
It is necessary for making up the order sheet. Write to:: US Dept. of Agriculture,
Agricultural Marketing Service, Fruit & Vegetable Division, Hunt's Point Market,
Room 4A, Bronx, NY 10474. Ask for the weekly FRESH FRUIT AND VEGETABLE MARKET NEWS.

MOTEL

Natural Brown Rice Lb	.50			
Whole Wheat Flour 5 Lb. Sack	1.52			
Deaf Smith P-Nut Butter 28 Oz.	1.48			
Granola 3 Lb. Sack	1.75			
Yogurt, Quart, Plain	.80			
			TOTAL	

BREAD SHOP

Sourdough Rye Bread 18 Oz.	.65			
Onion-White Bread 14 Oz.	.55			
Pumpernickel Bread 12 Oz.	.50			
Carrot Cake 11 Oz.	.65			
			Total	

CHICKEN LIVER (Hawaiian Style or Sweet and Sour: about 20 minutes preparation time)

1/4 cup butter or margerine
1 cup chopped celery
1/2 cup chopped onion
1 pepper sliced (not too wide)
1 1/2 lb. Chicken Livers

15 1/4 ounce can pineapple chunks, underlined drained
2 1/2 tablespoons brown sugar
1 tablespoon cornstarch
1 3/4 teaspoon salt
2 tablespoons cider vinegar

In a 12-inch skillet, melt fat. Using medium-high heat, cook celery, onion, pepper, until crisp tender – about 5 minutes – stir frying. Add chicken livers and cook for 10 minutes, stir frying. Add pineapple chunks. At the same time, you should have been preparing in a small bowl, as follows. Mix brown sugar, cornstarch, and salt. Gradually stir in vinegar and 3/4 cup water, stirring until smooth. Gradually stir this mixture into chicken livers and pineapple chunks, stirring constantly, until mixture is thickened. Serve with hot rice.

BRING BAGS TO MONDAY MEETINGS AND TO THURSDAY AND FRIDAY PICK-UP SITES.

There will be no coordinators meeting this Wednesday. Last week the 97th Street and House of Kuumba blocs were unrepresented. Remember if a bloc misses two consecutive meetings, then it will not be permitted to place food orders until it attends the next Wednesday Coordinator's meeting.

Turn in master orders on Tuesday nite between 6 and 8 PM. Telephone to find drop off point.

THURSDAY BLOCS: 864-8165

FRIDAY BLOCS: 865-8828

(Lost and found, use above numbers.)

There has been considerable discussion regarding our participation in the creation of a warehouse. You have received literature in the past. There is a committee at work trying to come up with a specific proposal that could be presented to us for approval or disapproval. In the interim, members are requested to pledge loans in anticipation of a vote to approve. This matter should be decided very soon.

MONEY SUMMARY

Produce	
X-LARGE BROWN EGGS	
Meat	
Dairy	
Peple's Resources	
Grain	
Bread	
SUB – TOTAL	
+ 5%	
SUB – TOTAL	
Credits	
NET CASH	

Bring bags to your Monday meetings and/or to the Thursday or Friday pick-up sites.

PEOPLES' MARKET UNION FOOD ORDER SHEET

Name _____

Address _____   Date _____

Phone _____

amount		min. order	cost	amount		min. order	cost
	GRAINS				**SEEDS**		
___	wheat hrw -------------	5 lb.	___	___	alfalfa -------------	1 lb.	___
___	brown rice sg ----------	1 lb.	___	___	pumpkin -------------	1 lb.	___
___	brown rice mg ----------	1 lb.	___	___	sesame --------------	1 lb.	___
___	millet ----------------	1 lb.	___	___	sunflower, hulled ---	1 lb.	___
___	barley, pearl ----------	1 lb.	___	___			___
___	yellow corn ------------	5 lb.	___				___
___	white corn -------------	5 lb.	___				
___	triticale --------------	5 lb.	___		**NUTS**		
___	popcorn ----------------	1 lb.	___	___	almonds, shelled ----	1 lb.	___
___			___	___	cashews -------------	1 lb.	___
___			___	___	pecans, shelled -----	1 lb.	___
				___	peanuts, shelled ----	1 lb.	___
	CEREALS			___	peanuts, roasted ----	1 lb.	___
___	wheat germ -------------	1 lb.	___	___	brazil --------------	1 lb.	___
___	rolled oats ------------	1 lb.	___	___	walnuts -------------	1 lb.	___
___	wheat flakes -----------	1 lb.	___	___	pistachios ----------	1 lb.	___
___	rye flakes -------------	1 lb.	___	___	nuts in shell -------	1 lb.	___
___	soy flakes -------------	1 lb.	___				
___	rice flakes ------------	1 lb.	___		**PASTA**		
___	bulghur wheat ----------	1 lb.	___	___	WW spaghetti --------	1 lb.	___
___			___	___	WW elbows -----------	1 lb.	___
				___	WW noodles ----------	1 lb.	___
	FLOURS						
___	whole wheat hrw --------	5 lb.	___		**HONEY**		
___	whole wheat pastry -----	5 lb.	___	___	local ---------------	1 lb.	___
___	unbleached white -------	5 lb.	___	___	commercial ----------	1 lb.	___
___	soy flour --------------	1 lb.	___				
___	yellow cornmeal --------	1 lb.	___		**OILS**		
___	white cornmeal ---------	1 lb.	___	___	corn ----------------	1 pt.	___
				___	safflower -----------	1 pt.	___
	BEANS			___	sesame --------------	1 pt.	___
___	blackeye peas ----------	1 lb.	___	___	soybean -------------	1 pt.	___
___	garbanzo ---------------	1 lb.	___	___	olive oil -----------	1 pt.	___
___	navy -------------------	1 lb.	___	___	peanut --------------	1 pt.	___
___	kidney -----------------	1 lb.	___	___	sunflower -----------	1 pt.	___
___	lentils, green ---------	1 lb.	___				
___	lentils, red split -----	1 lb.	___		**CONDIMENTS**		
___	lima, baby -------------	1 lb.	___	___	sea salt ------------	1 lb.	___
___	lima, large ------------	1 lb.	___	___	tamari --------------	1 lb.	___
___	mung beans -------------	1 lb.	___	___	miso ----------------	1 lb.	___
___	split peas -------------	1 lb.	___				
___	pinto ------------------	1 lb.	___		**FRUIT JUICE**		
___	soybeans ---------------	1 lb.	___	___	apple ---------------	1 gal.	___
___			___	___	grape ---------------	1 gal.	___

amount	DRIED FRUIT	min. order	cost	amount	POSSIBLY AVAILABLE VEGETABLES	min. order	cost
	raisins	1 lb.			artichokes	ea.	
	apples	1 lb.			mushrooms	lb.	
	apricots	1 lb.			parsley	bn.	
	peaches	1 lb.			turnips	lb.	
	prunes	1 lb.			greens	lb.	
	figs	1 lb.			eggplant	ea.	
	dates	1 lb.					

NUT BUTTER

	peanut, crunchy	1 lb.	
	peanut, smooth	1 lb.	
	sesame tahini	1 lb.	

FRESH FRUIT

	apples	ea.	
	avocadoes	ea.	
	bananas	1 lb.	
	oranges	ea.	
	grapefruit	ea.	
	lemons	ea.	
	limes	ea.	
	tangerines	ea.	
	pineapples	ea.	

CHEESE

	cheddar	lb.	
	swiss	lb.	
	monterey jack	lb.	
	mozzarella	lb.	
	longhorn	lb.	

FRESH VEGETABLES

EGGS

	grade A large	doz.	
	grade A med.	doz.	
	ungraded	doz.	

	FRESH VEGETABLES		
	broccoli	bn.	
	brussels sprouts	lb.	
	cauliflower	hd.	
	cabbage, green	hd.	
	cabbage, red	hd.	
	carrots	lb.	
	celery	bn.	
	corn	ea.	
	cucumbers	ea.	
	radishes	bag	
	garlic	oz.	
	onions	lb.	
	green onions	bn.	
	potatoes, red	lb.	
	potatoes, white	lb.	
	potatoes, sweet	lb.	
	lettuce, head	ea.	
	lettuce, leaf	bn.	
	romaine	bn.	
	spinach	lb.	
	pepper, green	ea.	
	squash, winter	ea.	
	squash, summer	ea.	
	squash, zucchini	ea.	

SURPLUS PURCHASES

	bread	lb.	
	powdered milk	lb.	
	butter	lb.	

SUB-TOTAL   A _____

% MARKUP --- (x A) B _____

SALES TAX (x A)   C _____

TOTAL (A+B+C) _____

All weights and measures will be
converted to <u>metric</u> as soon as
possible.

R.N.H. FOOD CO-OP

NAME_____ACCT #_____

DISTRIBUTION DATE_____

ORDERS MUST BE IN TO THE NEIGHBORHOOD HOUSE BY 4:30 P.M. TUESDAY WITH THE FULL AMOUNT OF PRUCHASE (CHECK ONLY) IN A SEALED ENVELOPE WITH YOUR ACC'T NUMBER ON THE FRONT. IDSTRIBUTION TAKES PLACE AT THE NEIGHBORHOOD HOUSE ON THURSDAY FROM 7-9P.M.

ITEM	SIZE	PRICE	QUANTITY	TOTAL
POTATOES, MAINE	5 lbs.		A	
POTATOES, IDAHO	5 lbs.		B	
ONIONS	1 lb.		C	
CARROTS	1 lb.		D	
APPLES	UNIT		E	
CUCUMBERS	UNIT		F	
GRAPEFRUIT	UNIT		G	
ORANGES	UNIT		H	
LEMONS	UNIT		I	
CELERY	STALK		J	
TOMATOES	1 lb.		K	
BANANAS	1 lb.		L	
STRINGBEANS	1 lb.		M	
BROCCOLI	Bunch		N	
PEPPERS	1 lb.		O	
LETTUCE	Head		P	
MUSHROOMS	lb.		Q	
PEARS	UNIT		R	
			S	
			T	
			U	
			V	
			W	
			X	
			Y	
			Z	
		TOTAL OF PRODUCE		
		TOTAL OF DAIRY		
		SUBTOTAL		
		CREDIT OR DEBIT		
		SURCHARGE		$.25
		TOTAL		

```
                          RNH CO-OP
                                Pick-up 1/30/75


Name_____     Account #_____


                       Meat and Dairy

  Item                              Size     Price    Quant.    Total

  American Slices                   1b.      1.00     A
  Valio Swiss                       1b.      1.19     B
  Muenster                          1b.      1.00     C
  Brie                              1b.      2.50     D
  Corn Oil Margarine                1b.       .83     E
  Butter-Salt                       1b.       .89     F
  Butter-Sweet                      1b.       .89     G
  Yogurt-Plain                      8 oz.     .26     H
  Yogurt-Flavored                   8 oz.     .29     I
  Friendship Cottage Cheese         16 oz.    .59     J
  Pepperidge Farm White Bread       2 1b.     .78     K
  Pepperidge Farm Pumpernickel      1b.       .46     L
  Pepperidge Farm Butter Rolls      12 pack   .48     M
  Arnold English Muffins            12 pack   .79     N
  Arnold Poppy Seed Rolls           10 pack   .52     O
                                            Dairy Total--------
  Riklin Smithfield Bacon           1b.      1.35     P
  Rib Roast 1st & 2nd Cuts          10 lbs.  14.00    Q
  Beef Stew                         3 lbs.    3.60    R
  Chicken Cutlets                   2 lbs.    3.40    S
  Lamb Chop Conbination rib, loin
                       shoulder     3 lbs.    4.50    T
  Foodwide Ground Sirloin           5 lbs.    6.50    U
  Paramount chickens                21/2-3lbs.1.30    V
  Chuck Steak Center Cut            2 lbs.    1.55    W
  Rib Steak                         1b.       1.55    X
                                                      Y
                                                      Z

  _____                        Meat Total--------
                                    Grand Total-------
                                    Bring forward to Page 1
```

Keeping Records

Whenever record-keeping is mentioned, financial records are
the type that usually comes to mind, but there are others that
have nothing to do with money; these will be discussed a bit
later in this section.

Small groups should keep their bookkeeping to a minimum; to do that, be certain that every single step of the bookkeeping process is completed at the end of every single transaction, on time.

The following is the basic formula for keeping the co-op's
financial record in order in the preorder/prepaid credits system:

total household orders, prepaid	minus	cost of foods and extra expenses	equals	surplus money
credits	plus	last week's cost of foods and extra expenses	equals	total household orders, prepaid
credits claimed this week		should equal		surplus money left over from last week

Simple? Well, don't forget that you may have a percentage markup on your order form or in your price calculations. If that's the case, you must adjust the totals by that percentage.

In a preorder/pay-on-delivery system, the record sheet looks like this:

first week's payments	minus	second week's food costs and expenses	leaves	kitty plus second week's payments
second week's payment plus kitty	minus	third week's food costs and expenses	leaves	kitty plus third week's payments

A comparison of [the total of the second week's payments and the kitty] to [the total of the third week's food costs plus expenses] will tell you how closely your week-to-week operations are running. Remember again that over several weeks, some members may miss one or two shopping cycles, so a strict week-to-week assessment is almost never possible.

Every receipt should be kept; you may need a receipt to figure out individual prices, to remember exactly which wholesalers you did business with, or to have proof of purchase if you need to return something or exchange something.

Tax regulations may require you to keep receipts. Food

stamp regulations in your city or state may require proof of purchase of the total dollar volume your group claims is being bought. The simplest and least costly method of filing these receipts, once the information has been obtained and used for the current shopping cycle, is to put them in a set of used envelopes marked with the date of distribution of the food purchased or with the name of the wholesaler.

Minutes of meetings are another form of record-keeping that can prove valuable. A discussion on new sources of foods would be of little use if no record exists of what the suggested sources were. In addition, when changes of policy, however slight, are instituted, there is then no question of exactly what the changes are, and when they were made. If the meeting place remains constant and the minutes-taker rotates, leave the minutes book at the meeting location. If the person remains constant and the meeting site rotates, keep the minutes book with the person.

I recommend keeping master shopping lists, for this reason. After a few cycles, survey what was ordered and in what quantities. Perhaps some items are sparsely ordered each time, and could be put on the list less often. This may result in a better price. For example, if the co-op orders about 25 pounds of split green peas each month, the two-month total would be about 50 pounds, making it possible to buy them in the 50-pound sack at a cheaper per pound price.

Work records should be kept only if (1) your group has adopted the work-credits system, or (2) it seems that some people are rarely doing any work. In either case, a record-keeping system that permits a member to record time worked in a master book kept by the coordinator should lead to the least-challenged set of records.

Satisfying Any Legal Requirements

Federal, state, or municipal laws pertaining to co-ops depend largely on what certain sets of law enforcement officials think that co-ops do. Some co-ops, using legal counsel, have clearly been set up as nonprofit organizations; others think of themselves as no formal organization at all, but simply as an extended-family type of operation. (There was a recent case in Missouri where a local official wanted a co-op to obtain a merchants' license, but the court ruled that the co-op was not selling but buying in a collective manner and then subdividing.) Whatever the actual situation, some local or state officials may see it a bit differently and ask you to comply with laws you may feel do not really apply. By far, the majority of co-ops never experience any problems, but the exception does occur, and it's best to be prepared.

A large number of co-ops, most in fact, especially small ones, and especially at the outset, do not incorporate, and have no need to do so. They simply conduct their business, cause no problems in their community, and roll along fine.

The only federal regulations you should become involved with are those of the Internal Revenue Service, and that would be for one of two reasons: first, if the co-op plans for any reason to incorporate, or must produce a tax-exempt certificate from the federal government to qualify for a state tax exemption; second, if your group plans to apply for authorization to accept food stamps from members. Currently, the IRS form needed for incorporating is Number 501 (c) (3), and it should be available at any office of the IRS or at information centers for federal agencies are usually located in the lobbies of all federal buildings. Food stamp information is found on page 116.

Many states have a state sales tax on food, and if you are in one of these (any food store manager will tell you), then you must obtain a sales tax exemption certificate or number. Contact the closest branch of the state sales tax office for details. State departments of public welfare may also be sources of information on this subject.

Plan to keep accurate, up-to-date records of your purchases in order to continue to qualify for this tax exemption, or to facilitate any other new development. Keep this in mind when setting up your money procedures. These records should include a list of members, a record of sales and volume, and the sources of supply. Also, in sales tax states, expect a visit from an inspector, who will be there to verify that it is indeed food for humans that the co-op is handling.

City or municipal ordinances should not be a problem to you unless you become a problem to someone else. There are recorded co-op incidents where food store owners or supermarket managers from across the street or down the block have put pressure on local officials to force a food co-op to comply with questionable regulations. The co-op may be asked by the city's Weights and Measures Department, for instance, to allow its scales to be tested for accuracy. Or a health code regulation requiring a butcher's license to be purchased, if any cutting of meats or cheeses is taking place, may be forced upon you. A city license exempting you from some zoning ordinance may be all they're after. Of course, the pressure is not always successful, and by and large this kind of harassment is rare. But the co-op should know about it, so if a problem of this sort appears, you can track down its source quickly.

If you choose to set up the limited partnership type of corporation or obtain a nonprofit organization status, you would need some legal counsel. The purposes or benefits of this move would be to allow the co-op to do things collectively, such as purchasing a shopping van or truck, or a refrigerator; to apply for fire, theft, or liability insurance; to get permission to use some space in a municipally owned building either for free or for a nominal rent; to qualify for accepting food stamps; or to deal with other organizations more easily.

Information needed for Articles of Incorporation includes:
1) co-op's official name and address,
2) co-op's purpose,
3) co-op's board of directors, and extent of their authority,
4) whether and how much stock will be issued.

Bylaws are usually written at the same time that the Articles are, and both should be prepared and approved by the members. Bylaws generally include information on the co-op's
1) name and location,
2) object as an organization,
3) structure,
4) membership requirements,
5) membership privileges and responsibilities,
6) general and special membership meetings,
7) finances,
8) amendment procedures for the bylaws

With the aid of a lawyer, the articles are filed with the state (the filing fee is usually not very much—$10–$15 range). Ask the lawyer whether the word "co-op" may legally be used in the group's official name. If you'd like some ideas on the exact structure and wording of food co-op Articles and Bylaws that meet the standards for your state, contact the nearest regional information center, listed in Appendix D, and ask them to match you with a co-op that can be of assistance. Legal advice may be obtained free from a Legal Aid office, the law school of some universities, the office of some local, state, and national politicians, community service agency staffs, or a co-op member who is also a lawyer. Be certain it is the correct information for the situation, and that the lawyer understands exactly what the group's position and needs are.

The two most sound bits of advice in any discussion of legal compliance are: don't accept amateur advice if you find yourself needing some information; keep all correspondence from all government agencies, along with copies of your letters and forms sent to them.

And if it all gets too awesome to deal with, I advise that you keep your sense of humor and improvise.

Food Stamps Only after the co-op has been operating for a few cycles can it consider starting the procedure necessary to accept food stamps from members who receive them as payment. The complexity of this procedure depends on where in the country and where in the state you live. It is not the easiest part of the food co-op process, but it is well worth the group's time and energy if the co-op is going to serve fully its members' food and financial needs.

Authorization to accept food stamps is determined by your local United States Department of Agriculture Food Stamp office. The requirements they expect a food co-op to meet depend on your location. To begin with, wherever you are, the group must become incorporated as a nonprofit organization. This is neither a complicated nor a costly procedure, but it definitely requires the services of a lawyer. Make every attempt to get those services donated, through Legal Aid Society staff members, a community service agency, the office of a local, state, or national politician, or a friend.

Then the co-op must file an application with the Internal Revenue Service to obtain federal tax exempt status. Your nearest IRS office will mail you the form which, once filled out, should take about two weeks to process (twice as long between January 1 and the end of April). You will then have a certificate from the IRS that the co-op is officially recognized as a nonprofit organization.

On the state tax office level, the procedure is much the

same, except that your IRS certificate is used to obtain the state nonprofit recognition certificate. In some states and cities, you can proceed directly, with your two certificates, to the USDA Food Stamp Office.

In other states, and particularly in the cities in those states, your second certificate will be used to obtain a third one, this from the city tax office.

Three copies of the co-op's Bylaws, plus information on where and when the food is distributed, plus written assurance that absolutely no food is stored overnight on the premises, are then filed with the city health inspector's office or the city health department. They will issue you a health permit. An inspector will drop around to be sure that what you said on paper takes place in real life.

These four—federal, state, city, and health—certificates are finally presented to the USDA Food Stamp Office, which issues the co-op an authorization card, or license, and special IBM bank deposit slips to use for depositing the food stamps into a bank account. The card may be used in purchasing foods with the food stamps directly from wholesalers authorized to accept them. Or else your group can "process" the food stamps by depositing them in a bank account, which, in effect, turns them into operating cash. However, the actual details of this bank process are often left to the individual bank, which may require the co-op to use a commercial bank account or to hold its food stamps outside the bank until $100 worth of stamps have accumulated, at which time it will accept a deposit. If the bank's regulations become too restrictive, inquire at the Food Stamp Office about their ability to modify or soften the regulations. If they can't or won't, change banks.

This authorization must be updated yearly, so keep all the necessary correspondence, forms, and records in good order.

Food stamps may be used by the co-op to purchase any food for human consumption, but be certain you don't jeopardize your authorization and some people's source of food by using them for pet foods, paper products, or other nonfood items that an inspector would frown on.

Ask the Food Stamp Office to please keep the co-op informed of any pending changes in policy of any sort, and extend every effort to comply with all its policies.

Overall, the whole process may take a few months. See if one or two of the group's more punctual, good-with-details members might volunteer to become a special Food Stamp Launching Committee. Perhaps the rest of the group will exempt these members from some of the more involved tasks while they handle this important project. In the long run, it's a valuable, worthwhile investment to facilitate some members' use of the full benefits of the co-op.

Part IV: Evaluating and Adjusting Your Co-op

After you've been operating for a few buying cycles, hold a meeting to evaluate how each step in your overall system is working. Remind members that it is not unusual for a problem to spring up during formative weeks, and that it's advisable to accept the idea calmly and concentrate on correcting the flaws that appear in the co-op's system.

If you make allowances for the process of learning a new way of doing things, ask yourself just how smoothly the functions are being carried out.

Here are some key questions for the group to ask itself after a few shopping trips have been completed:

1) Are you saving *at least* 20 percent on the foods the co-op is handling?

2) Are the finances holding their own from cycle to cycle, approximately?

3) Are people able to pick up their filled-out grocery order within fifteen minutes after they arrive at the co-op's distribution center?

4) Are there any major disagreements over what responsibilities go with which jobs?

5) Is any one person always "in charge"?

6) Is any one part of the overall system far more difficult for the members to adjust to than expected?

If the answers to questions 1, 2, and 3 are Yes and to 4, 5, and 6 are No, your group is in fine shape. If not, here are some considerations to study:

1) If the group is not saving at least 20 percent, you may be paying out more than you can afford. You may not be buying in large enough bulk or wholesale quantities, and might consider listing some items less frequently, so that when they are available each household places a larger order. You may have chosen some foods that sell very close to the wholesale price at retail supermarkets, and bring in their profit to the supermarket through volume and fast turnover, or else are placed in supermarkets as "Loss Leader" items (bargains to lure customers in who then purchase other goods). Or your wholesaler may be overcharging you. Investigate prices of comparable foods from other wholesalers, and either demand equally low prices or switch.

2) If the finances are not holding their own from cycle to cycle, examine just what amount of money the discrepancy is. If it's a few pennies or a dollar, perhaps you might increase the markup by an extra percent, or raise the surcharge 5¢, or whatever system your group uses to cover additional expenses. If you're actually losing serious money, immediately trace back every transaction during the previous two shopping cycles (here's an example of the value of keeping records and receipts). Compare checks and receipts. Check whether anyone has taken credit for food they actually received. Trace the flow of cash, step by step. Institute a double-check system to oversee the arithmetic on order forms at the point where money is collected. And above all, involve all members in this process. Everyone must know if there's a financial crisis, and must be involved in its solution. If not, others will feel that (a) detailed money matters are not something for everyone to care or learn about, (b) a few people will always handle the troubleshooting or (c) some sneaky covering up is going on, and they'll decide to drop out without learning whatever it is that actually happened.

3) If members must wait longer than fifteen minutes to receive their filled-out order, see if these conditions are being met:

a) They are being told a realistic time to arrive. For example, if packing always takes about an hour, and begins about 6 P.M., don't encourage anyone who is not on the packing crew to arrive before 7. An overoptimistic estimate of 6:45 will not only annoy someone who has scheduled other stops with the assumption that orders would be ready at that time, it could also disrupt the packing crew's work, causing further delays.

b) The "traffic pattern" at the co-op's distribution center is not well planned. If your group's distribution point has two exits, design your packing operation's floor plan with this in mind, so that people enter through one door (and pay, if that's part of your system, or leave off empty bags and egg cartons), and exit with their food by the door closer to the parking area or the street. If there's only one door, try to separate the functions that go on, moving everything else *away* from the door, leaving it clear for members exiting with bags, boxes, and shopping carts of food. It will be helpful, for example, to post information for all members to read on the wall farthest away from the door. Once people learn what and where it is (such as the sheets listing shortages and surplus), they will walk to it.

c) If too many people are arriving in a short span of time, the group might consider adding an extra fifteen minutes to the pickup period to prevent congestion and resulting confusion.

d) Packing may need to be better organized if the allotted time lengthens appreciably with any slight change in foods ordered or in the makeup of the packing crew. Check to see if the packing crew is actually following the prearranged system. Often people will skip steps in an attempt to save an extra minute, and then make an error that takes twenty minutes to unravel. For instance, a packing crew member may not check to see if a particular item has been bought by the pound or by the piece (such as green peppers) and may pass out five green peppers when five pounds were ordered, and so on. At the end, a huge "surplus" of green peppers will "appear." The packer will then have to remove all the green peppers from all the bags, and begin again.

e) Delays in packing may also result if the packing crew needs but does not have sufficient bags, waxed paper, etc.

4) Disagreements about exactly what is involved in each job must be cleared up as soon as they emerge, and they must be settled by the group. This can develop into a serious sore point if not checked at the beginning, and reevaluated from time to time. Remember, as people know how the whole co-op

functions, they will evolve helpful, clever refinements within each job. Just be sure that these improvements are shared with the group, or else whenever the person who instituted them is absent, they will not be put into practice. For instance, a woman in our group devised a clever, unmessy way of dividing up a 6-pound block of cheese into one-pound chunks. She takes a strip of waxed paper or newspaper as long as the cheese, and folds it into thirds, and then again in half, giving her six equal portions. She then uses the strips of folded paper as a cutting guide; members have been very pleased with the precise, non-ragged pounds of cheese they've been receiving. If she did not explain this "system" to others, we'd be back to our sloppy, eye-approximate chunks whenever she's not on the packing crew.

5) Creeping maternalism/paternalism is one of a co-op's greatest hidden killers. While it seems comfortable for one person to be involved in every stage of the game, it lets the co-op wide open for collapse if that person is removed from the scene for any reason (illness, moving away, vacation, death, or simply dropping out). If a few people who initially get things rolling do not avoid this possible development, they will soon find themselves in a position of too much responsibility. They must insist that others serve often or at least learn how to serve as coordinators, cashiers, tabulators, and shoppers, so that the information and the experience will be spread around.

6) Continual complaints or dissatisfaction about one specific step in the whole process probably means the co-op is not adequately serving the needs of its members and a change should be made. In that case, ask members how things might be rearranged to eliminate that common problem. We're talking, again, about serious problems, not merely inconveniences.

If the hours when members pick up their food are a serious problem, another volunteer job might be added, asking someone to wait around an extra hour or two with the food.

If the day when members pick up their food is a serious problem, the shopping day may need to be changed. Keep in mind that some wholesale distributors are not open every day, so that you must adjust several things when moving the shopping day.

If the time or day when orders are placed is a serious problem, review the other systems described. Perhaps a different system of ordering might be instituted, one that you now feel would suit the group better than the one you originally chose.

If getting volunteers for all the jobs is a serious problem, those that are doing the work must call a special meeting and express their dissatisfaction with the consequence. Either a new system must be adopted (perhaps with more accountability) or members who have continually shirked responsibility should be given the choice of working or dropping out. It's far better to lose one or two members who are ordering but not working than to permit resentment to build up. If the problem of getting enough household orders to make up a wholesale quantity makes the group wary of losing those lazy members, you might either (a) order those items less frequently, so that each household places a larger order when it is available, or (b) find another co-op within a reasonable distance and split an order with them, or (c) find a few new members.

Decisions on Growth

As the word gets out that a new food co-op has begun to function, the members will be approached by other people interested in joining. Once the co-op and its original members have launched their buying/paying/working system somewhat successfully, the group should discuss the following issues:

1) Is there a "next level" of growth the group wants to limit itself to?

2) Should new members be restricted to people known to someone in the co-op already, or is the co-op functioning well enough that new people could be integrated with little disruption?

3) Will the same initial membership fee paid by the original members be charged new members?

4) How can new members be educated about exactly how the co-op runs?

5) Would new members expect a different selection of foods?

6) Would all members, new and old, then do less volunteer work for each buying period, or would the group divide into work teams?

7) Are there any special skills or equipment that have

been offered by potential new members which would alter or simplify the existing way of running things?

8) Would new members be subject to a trial period?

If the group is happy with its present size, perhaps new people could be encouraged to create their own food co-op with a little help and guidance from you. Many, many co-ops are doing splendidly with a stable membership of twenty and under, and are quite content never to grow any larger.

If the group, however, sees added benefits in accepting new members, it should address itself, beyond the points listed above, to what may appear to be a more drastic roadblock than it actually is—space limitations.

Artificial Boundaries Limits of space may appear to determine the size to which the co-op can grow. Here's a quick look at the three common places where a set space appears to dictate the upper limit of membership.

1) The distribution center. If the space the group uses for packing and distributing seems to be just large enough for the food bought for the current members, take a more careful look at that space. Could a second level of work surface be obtained with the addition of old kitchen tables or doors on sawhorses placed against all the walls? Perhaps shelving or countertops, built inexpensively from recycled wood by some of the members, could increase the carrying capacity. Or else alternate sites might be suggested or investigated, maybe by someone eager to join the co-op.

2) The shopping vehicle. If the car, station wagon, or van you use for the shopping trip seems filled to near overflowing now, you might consider using a second vehicle. Does the shopping vehicle make stops at two or three suppliers before returning to the co-op distribution point? Making two trips might solve the overcrowding problem.

A larger group and the resulting larger orders may now qualify the co-op for having some items delivered by distributors. If so, that frees some additional space in the shopping vehicle. A larger membership may also permit the co-op to purchase larger bulk quantities of produce and dried goods, which may come in one bulk container and not necessarily take up twice as much room for twice as much food. One 100-pound sack would take up less space than four 25-pound sacks, for instance.

3) The order form. Some groups are apprehensive about adding new members because new members bring new food requests, and they don't want to wind up with a crowded, hard-to-read and hard-to-fill out order form. The most common solution is to use two pages, or else to use the front and back of one sheet. Just be certain that the expanded version meets the requirements of the cashier, the tabulator, the packing crew, and anyone else who uses the order form as part of their volunteer job. Including the date at the top of the order form becomes even more important if each household must now use two separate sheets of paper. Consider labeling them A and B or use some other method to provide an added reminder that each order should consist of two forms.

After all these possible readjustments have worked themselves out, it's advisable to rewrite the descriptions of jobs and to distribute copies to each member. Be certain that everyone realizes there is a new, revised job-descriptions list and does not refer to the old list by mistake. Take this opportunity to list the names, addresses, and telephone numbers of all co-op members in case there have been any changes since the first membership list was compiled and passed out. Include any other information pertinent to the co-op—for example, the full, correct mailing address the co-op is using, pickup location and hours, and work and meeting schedules, if any.

Throughout this stage of evaluation and change, keep in mind that the group is building its own special system that should work and function in response to the co-op's needs. Later, as weeks go by, think of additional readjustments as the fine tuning of an already-running well-constructed piece of machinery, or else as the delicate subtle seasonings in a fine soup recipe, once the basics of that recipe have been mastered.

Growing Through New Members

Once the co-op has smoothed out the organizational wrinkles and decided to accept a substantial number of new members, the group should plan on how to treat them and what to expect from them.

During the early stages, a few new members will have joined. This current influx would be people who were asked to wait a few weeks, while the co-op re-evaluated its work-paying-buying pattern and stabilized it.

First, give prospective new members a thorough briefing on how the co-op's buying/paying/work system operates, and explain how they will have to fit into this particular pattern. If they are unable to make the adjustments necessary, suggest that they either contact another food co-op in the region or else form a new group that would be tailored to serve their own special requirements.

Second, tell them if the group has decided on a trial period for new members. Explain what membership fee the group has agreed on, and exactly what happens to that money.

Third, invite them to an ordering meeting, a packing crew session, or anything else that could convey the flavor of how the co-op runs.

Fourth, be certain that no new member is matched to a job that requires special skills or information. Pair a new member with an old member for a few weeks, letting the new member learn jobs that require two people. Gradually the other jobs and their importance will become clear, and then the new member can be matched to one of them.

Fifth, let the new members join right in on the workings, benefits, obligations, and processes of the co-op. Treat them as full members, and assume they will work out as good members from the start. The trust that was present among the original members must be extended to new members, and it must come from the group, and extend outward to the new people.

Fitting Them into Your System New members should have an overall idea of how the co-op works so they themselves can determine the most effective way to fit into the group's system. Don't expect a new member to take over a job or a responsibility simply because the time he or she joined coincides with the time a vacancy occurred in a particular job.

Avoid altering the basic scheduling of steps to suit new members. Any constructive suggestions on procedure, sources of supply, or methods of distribution—even from a rank novice—should be welcomed and discussed by all the membership. Just remember how important it is to keep intact the system you have worked out so carefully and which has shown to work well for its users.

New members should join old members in the formation of

standing committees, which would aim to streamline even further the co-op operations. Some possible designations for committees are education, membership, financial, and newsletter.

The education committee keeps the members abreast of all policy changes so that each person understands the workings of the co-op. Someone from this committee could record the minutes from special and general meetings, and maintain an accurate, up-to-date description of every facet of the co-op's operations, from job descriptions to the fastest, least complicated car route to the wholesale market. Outside groups seeking to establish a co-op of their own, patterned in some ways after yours or else using some of your sources and procedures, could be referred to the education committee.

Membership committee responsibilities generally start when a co-op decides on a definite goal of increasing its membership in a specific way. For example, a co-op may wish to insure that it will have a certain number of members during the summer months, when some people would be away. Or they may wish to add new members only from within their own apartment building, church group, or neighborhood. The committee would then launch a specific drive to achieve these goals. The membership committee should also oversee the introduction of new members to the co-op, not only by name, but also by explaining step by step how the co-op works. Perhaps a flow chart and a printed job-descriptions list would assist them in this activity.

The financial committee could oversee the monetary transactions of the group, including a monthly review of income and expenditures. If membership fees are refundable in your group, this committee could keep an accurate record of these collections and repayments. It could also handle the paperwork involved in obtaining clearance for using food stamps, in filing any tax returns when required, and in gathering comparative prices for equipment or services the co-op needs.

The newsletter committee could produce a simple duplicated or mimeographed publication, using the same equipment that is utilized in producing the order form. It could be available monthly, every other week, four to six times a year, or whenever the committee and the members feel it should come out. Besides announcing changes of policy that the education committee has recorded and written out, the newsletter could print the schedules of regular and special meetings, convey information about other co-ops in the region, relate information about the national food co-op movement, suggest recipes for some of the foods the co-op buys or is planning to try, invite reactions and suggestions from members, and generally help to create a sense of community among all the people in the co-op. Distribute the newsletter with each household's food, or else make it available with the order forms.

Your group may decide that only one, or two, or none of these committees has a place in the co-op as it now exists. A special committee to deal with a particular situation, such as redesigning the distribution center, or selling surplus food, may be chosen. Or you may decide that these committees might do different or additional functions than those listed.

A committee can comprise only two people and do a very effective job. For instance, the newsletter committee might be the secretary and one other person. The financial committee might be whoever signs checks and whoever does tabulating often. Don't let the word "committee" lead you into establishing something far too overblown for the purpose. At all times, the co-op is a collection of people sharing work and energy to help each other, not a power structure laden with people designated by title instead of first name.

Finally, the group must decide how time spent on committees fits into the regular cycle-to-cycle time requirements members must meet to fulfill their personal co-op responsibilities and to keep the co-op running. Be certain you don't wind up with people too engrossed in these committees, while the real purpose of the group—the creation and operation of a food co-op—slowly deteriorates because everyone feels that (a) it's no longer their job to do the "routine" work, or (b) someone else will do it. You may find yourself confronted by a new member coming into the group and asking, "Who's minding the co-op?"

Growing Through New Items

Whether the co-op expands its membership or not, the group will more than likely wish to add more selections to the order form.

In the early part of the book, my recommendation was to

begin with produce; many co-ops begin with other foods instead, or with only two or three categories of foods your group may be already buying from these other categories. If not, refer back now to the information on researching other kinds of wholesalers.

It would be wise to reread the section on What Foods Your Group Wants, because you should learn exactly what new types of foods the co-op will be able to purchase in bulk. Moreover, members who joined after the initial research stage did not have an opportunity to list their preferences beyond the basic list.

More Produce It is now possible to increase the number of fresh fruits and fresh vegetables on your order form. This assumes, of course, that the co-op would be buying the additional produce at the same location and with the same arrangements as the original produce list.

If not, review the section on researching produce sources of supply. Also, consider the implications of a second produce shopping trip. Unlike the other categories, fresh produce must be checked for quality and freshness as well as price each time it is listed on the order form, since it is purchased at the market, where shoppers must compare before they buy. Therefore, a second-stop to buy produce could add much more time to that job of shopping than many people may be able to devote. Additional items bought at the same wholesale market, however, do not add an overwhelmingly greater burden on the shoppers. This might be the opportunity to add produce that only a few members might want, but these must come in small numbers per carton, such as avocadoes or mushrooms.

Farmer's market sections of the wholesale market should be visited regularly during the months when farmers bring their produce to the market for sale. Contacting farmers in advance and asking to arrange with them some ongoing deals would definitely be worth doing. The information on contacting farmers is found in the research section, but it should be mentioned here that the time when the co-op considers expanding its food choices on the order form is a good time to investigate how best to purchase fresh fruits and vegetables from area farmers whenever possible. Farmers might also lower their prices even more if the co-op supplies its own baskets, boxes, or crates.

Modifying Your System When the Group Doubles, Triples and Quadruples

The size your co-op grows to is completely in the hands of the original members, and if the group decides at the outset that it will accept only ten more members, then that's the size and no more!

If a ceiling is placed on the number of members, perhaps the group might consider creating a waiting list of people who will be permitted to replace those who move away or drop out for any reason. A waiting list has been known to serve as a useful reminder to co-op members that should they decide not to pull their own fair share of the responsibilities, someone else will always be more than happy to join the co-op in their place.

Most small co-ops can double in size with no basic changes in their patterns of operation. As mentioned in the sections on work, money and distribution systems, it's possible to divide up volunteer jobs into component parts or functions, so each person actually does half as much work as before. For instance, in a meeting-type operation, one person may now be verifying arithmetic on order sheets and also collecting money and making correct change. These two functions can be split, and each person would then do half as much work. Or else a second person can be matched to a job, such as tabulating, now done by only one person, cutting in half the actual time required for that job's completion.

As discussed in Artificial Boundaries, the group must examine how growth affects the various steps in the operation and plan alternate methods of handling any of the problems that may result.

Groups that triple and quadruple in size will need to make serious plans about handling the real increase in volume, time, and procedures that will result. Some groups decide to split into two, starting a whole new co-op with some veteran members and some newer ones. Or else they may decide to do everything separately except preparing the order forms and shopping, which would give all the members of both groups the advantage of lower prices through increased bulk-quantity purchases. But their food distribution would be done separately, with the shoppers leaving off food at two different points.

And their ordering time and place or procedure would be separate, perhaps governed by geography or the schedules of the members.

When there is a move to increase the membership threefold or fourfold, this is the best time to reexamine the section on handling the work. Perhaps a system that looked unattractive at the earlier stages of the group's operation may now seem suited to it, now that its size will be increased.

Also, you may wish to stay with your present system but divide the group into teams, with each team totally able to carry on the operations of the co-op. In adopting this solution, the system that everyone has created will continue, and members would only do volunteer jobs half as often, or even one-third as often.

If the co-op grows to four times its original size, the thought of maintaining a checking account at a local bank may now hold more merit. Refer back to the Cash vs. Check section for additional points to consider on that subject.

Remember again the value of reexamining some of the decisions that were made early on, before the co-op had been running as smoothly. A decision then to limit the size of the membership may have been the result of the original members wanting things to stabilize and not get too unwieldy. Now, with your buying/work/money system off and running, the thought of new members, more foods, and slight alterations in the procedure should be far less intimidating.

Federating or Sharing with Other Co-ops

It's helpful to new co-ops and buying clubs to know how far along others have progressed, what's possible for them, and that if they collectively choose to do so, they can plug into an ongoing national food co-op movement.

Chicago's Food Co-op Project, listed in Appendix D, can tell you how to contact other co-ops in your region. You may discover a willingness to combine orders for certain items from time to time. For instance, some members of your group may be strongly interested in obtaining soy sauce and others may not; result—never enough orders to create a bulk amount, a case of 24 bottles. A near-by co-op may be experiencing the same difficulty, with no resolution in sight either. A combined order between the two groups could give you both the necessary 24 orders. After some minor negotiations, one group agrees to arrange for the ordering of the case of soy sauce, the other agrees to handle the pickup and delivery. Intergroup cooperation is born!

Just such deals among individual groups often lead to a federation in which a few groups decide to order from the same order form, buy all the food at once, and then subdivide the bulk order into each co-op's order.

Consider what changes take place in an arrangement like this. First, the physical workload is somewhat reduced for all involved, since only one shopping trip is required instead of, for example, four trips, but the time needed in tabulating and distributing orders is increased.

Each group must accept the fact that their direct participation in the actual, personal selection of the food will be reduced or cut back to one out of every four times if four groups federate. Decisions on exactly what is offered for purchase by members may also be reduced if each co-op takes a turn at preparing the new order form.

Each group must accept the fact that accountability, at least the personal kind involving people they know, would be lost three out of every four times.

These changes would occur if the four groups simply rotate the "heavy work" among each co-op. This means that Group A would collect the master shopping lists from Groups B, C, and D, tabulate them into a giant list, arrange for the purchase and pickup of all the foods, subdivide them into each co-op's order, and prepare a new order form. The following week, B would run through the cycle, and A would merely order their food and deal with its own internal co-op's order, once the food has been subdivided for it. Each co-op handles its own food distribution it did before.

The alternative method of federating or affiliating with other co-ops is for each step of the operation to be handled by some members of each group. Assuming there are four groups again, in this system, one member from each group would be responsible for helping to tabulate the master order; another all-group team would do the shopping and pickup of preordered foods, while a third team would subdivide the total bulk order into each co-op's order, and so on.

As with all the other systems presented in this book, variations are possible. For example, tabulating, shopping, and order-form preparation could rotate among all the groups, handled by one group at a time, but subdividing the bulk order of food into four co-op orders might always be handled by a team of one or two members from each co-op working together.

Co-op Warehouses as Supply Sources In some cities, warehouses have been formed by independent member co-ops joining together to organize a space for storage until each co-op picks up its part of the order or as a bulk buying facility. This helps co-ops to combine their orders for certain foods to make them all eligible for even lower prices, since purchasing at the same time usually means the bulk order is delivered at the same time.

This does not mean that all the food that co-op warehouses handle must be stored for long periods. In some cases, member co-ops pool their produce order, and after it's purchased and delivered to the warehouse, they can pick it up that same day.

A warehouse may also be a co-op's best or only source of supply for certain items. Affiliation with a co-op warehouse may make it possible for your co-op to add certain items it would otherwise be unable to locate or to garner a bulk amount for.

Group action like this among co-ops in recent years has grown from an occasional sharing of an order with a neighborhood co-op to some highly structured, sophisticated operations, including collective dealings with cross-country truckers and joint ownership and staffing of warehouses. If a co-op warehouse is operating near you (at a distance close enough to drive to in a reasonable amount of time), your co-op should consider that warehouse as a source of supply, as you would a wholesale food distributor. The people at the co-op warehouse may be easier to deal with, more flexible in their scheduling, and more willing to locate specific items for you. To locate the warehouse closest to you, write or contact the regional information center or largest food co-op in your region, listed in Appendix D in zip code order.

If you do locate a warehouse close enough to deal with,

explain your money-handling and shopping systems to some-one there. As with any other distributor, you need to learn when you may pick up your foods, if they deliver and for what additional charge, what quantities they deal in, how items and price changes can be learned, and whether they require a minimum order or a membership fee of any kind. Sometimes co-ops can be eligible for a greater discount if they agree to supply volunteer labor for a certain number of hours per month. Some warehouses expect or encourage members to serve on an advisory committee which administers the business and policies of the warehouse.

Your group may want to talk with someone from another co-op which buys from the warehouse about the merits and advantages of using it. Whatever degree of involvement your group chooses, I advise retaining other sources of supply for foods the warehouse does not carry. If not, your members may lose touch with the concept of direct participation, and many co-ops fold up as soon as operations get too regimented and/or too simple. The constant input of activity is what keeps co-ops alive and healthy.

Sharing Information with Other Co-ops Shared information is as valuable as shared work to small co-ops in the same region. While your co-op may settle into a comfortable pattern of ordering, buying, and working with a set of number of members, do not overlook the benefits of tracking down neighborhood or regional groups to exchange sources of supply, organizational ideas, and facts about foods of the area.

Beyond the easily discovered or intently tracked-down sources of wholesale purchase, it is not unusual for an individual member of a co-op to know someone at a wholesale distribution organization, and to develop that organization as a source of supply based on that personal relationship. This exact situation could exist in a near-by co-op, and lead to a new source for your group, one you wouldn't have any other way of uncovering.

Information about regional farmers may also be secured this way. Their location, availability, reliability, and individual traits are better learned from a food co-op that has already had dealings with them.

Part V: Co-op Community

The fun and excitement of creating something like a food co-op lies partly in discovering new friends and new sides of old friends. Too often, we conduct our lives within a closed circle, unwilling or unable to open that circle even the slightest bit. A food co-op lets in some outside life.

More often than not, people who create and build a new food co-op find there are other interests and activities they can share, and all benefit from the increased involvement and participation. The most common activities are those that begin as part of the co-op operation, and then gain separate lives of their own.

On my block, many families with children had a parent who could volunteer to work on the packing crew during mid-afternoon only if a sitter could be found for the children. The co-op decided to create the volunteer job of sitter, and now each week one person watches the children of the others, freeing them to work on the packing crew for an hour.

Other groups have witnessed the expansion of this process. Once people meet each other and trust their children to each other for an hour each week, they decide to extend that to a regular system of rotating baby-sitting for a few hours each weekday. For instance, five different parents can each take a weekday morning and watch all the children one day apiece. This leaves four other mornings free for doing those things more easily done without children. The Mountain Co-op, listed in Appendix A, now has a preschool co-op that got its start through the food co-op, and is now independently run.

Many, many groups, especially in rural co-ops, decide to combine regular meetings with potluck suppers, where each household prepares and brings one dish, and everyone shares all the food. This is an excellent solution to the problem of members getting together early in the evening for a meeting, which might mean having to skip or delay dinner. It also serves as a pleasant way for new members to meet older ones in a social setting. (At least one "couple" in every co-op worth anything has met during the packing, the shopping, the potluck suppers, or the garbage removal. Actual statistics are unavailable, but it's commonly felt that they are higher than comparable supermarket statistics!)

Potluck suppers can also be a welcome solution to the problem of organizing a long meeting. The preliminaries can be presented while everyone is eating, and the detailed discussion can take place afterward. (A collection of 50¢ per household, or 35¢ per person in attendance, could help finance the inexpensive pocket calculator and the tabulator that shoppers have been requesting.)

Acting on the principle that throwing money away is to be discouraged, some groups have initiated a practice common to large families—a free coupon exchange within their co-ops. Members bring discount redemption coupons from packages, newspapers, and magazines, advertising campaigns through the mail, or other sources that they can't use personally, and leave them where the order forms are, or where the food is picked up, or near the cashier at the meeting. Members who can use them simply take the ones they want and leave others. There's no rule that you must leave some to get some. People only take what they can use, leave the rest, return the courtesy by offering into circulation all coupons they don't want. Periodically, someone goes through the coupons and removes the ones that have expired. Some co-ops who employ this extra device for cooperative exchanging of money-saving coupons do not limit the coupons to food, but offer any coupons they feel other members might find valuable.

These three activities—baby-sitting pools, potluck suppers, and coupon exchanges—are direct results of or additions to a co-op's regular operations. Many other mutually helpful activities have sprung up because a collection of people have met each other through a cooperative situation.

Not related directly to the running of the co-op but directly connected with the topic of food is better nutrition. Often co-ops will include health tips on their order forms or in their newsletter. Interest in better nutrition, usually sparked by some members' use of more fresh produce and more dried, natural foods, is channeled into nutrition classes or workshops. Some co-ops maintain a standing nutrition committee to inform members of healthful recipes and news about nutrition; others invite nutritionists, organic foods experts or food consumer reporters to speak at meetings, classes, or forums for members. Often this interest also translates into the addition of certain new items onto the order form.

Another large series of activities that commonly grow out of food co-ops are the other types of cooperatively organized, membership-run groups. Credit unions, consumer education groups, bicycle co-ops, car pools, community garages, carpentry collectives, and tenants' associations are all run by their members in much the same manner as food co-ops. (Of course, some of these groups may find themselves sponsoring a food co-op, using regular members and their existing organizational structure as a base.) And time after time, the good feeling, the sense of being able to make a group effort produce positive results, and an understanding of the process of creating and building such an organization have led to the formation of all these types of organizations. Particulars differ from type to type, naturally, and from group to group. But the process is basically the same, and once it's understood, any of these and other groups can be created.

Finally, better neighborhoods, closer associations with the people who live in your community, and a keener awareness of your immediate surroundings are all traceable by-products of what happens when you know more people on the block, or in your neighborhood, or when people from other co-ops in your area get together with you and your fellow members. Each member can broaden his or her circle of personal acquaintances, getting more benefit from the community. And that community can be an apartment building in New York City, an area on the south side of Chicago around a neighborhood church, a college section of Austin or a sixty-mile area in rural Arkansas. Cooperating makes for communicating, and both are useful, welcome tools in these changing, textured times.

Appendix A

Co-op Descriptions and Flow Charts

On the following pages are descriptions and flow charts of six different co-ops, some small and some large. The large co-ops, however, all began with a membership of twelve or less. A coordinator or active member from each food co-op also provides some comments and advice.

In consulting the flow charts, notice how different parts of each system work. Follow the flow of the money through each chart; follow the flow of order forms and information used to make up new ones; follow the time sequence from step to step.

Name	**Whipple Co-op**
Location	**Rochester, New York**
Money System	**Preorder/Pay-on-Delivery**
Distribution System	**Teams**
Work System	**Regular and Rotating Jobs**
Types of Foods	**Dried Goods, Natural Foods**
Sources of Foods	**Clear Eye Warehouse**
Ordering Cycle	**Monthly**

"Last September we moved to university housing," wrote Steve and Patti Zimmer, "and put up a notice inviting people to form a co-op. Membership stands at 25–30 families, with usual university turnover. New members are charged 50 cents to join. Orders and distribution are made on a monthly basis. Minimum quantities are 5 lbs. or 1 gallon . . . Presently we buy almost exclusively from Clear Eye.

"Orders are tallied and distributed on a rotating basis. Two members share a given job and one of the pair is replaced the following month. Order blanks are distributed near the end of the month and must be returned to the talliers by a given

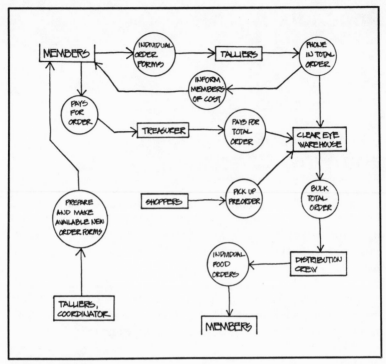

Whipple Food Co-op
Rochester, New York

deadline. The talliers try to fill as many individual orders as possible in trying to make up the bulk order. After checking with Clear Eye as to which items are still in stock, they place the order and then notify members as to the price of their respective order. Checks and containers must be received by a deadline and orders must be picked up within three days of bagging by the distributors or the member forfeits the food.

"The co-op is loosely run—on purpose, perhaps, so that it might survive the turnover of its members and founders . . . complaints are helpful in establishing guidelines for a workable co-op."

Important to them is the fact that "so many people are naive about the use of basic foodstuffs and even when aware, prefer quick-preparing supermarket food, which is, for the most part, nutritionally inferior to what Clear Eye has to offer. In order to get people interested in the more basic foods, recipes are distributed monthly along with the order blanks. Usually the recipes involve complementing vegetable proteins à la *Diet for a Small Planet*."

Name	**Mountain Co-op**
Location	**East Stroudsburg, Pennsylvania**
Money System	**Preorder/Prepaid**
Distribution System	**Teams**
Work System	**Teams**
Types of Foods	**Dried Goods, Natural Foods, Some Produce**
Sources of Foods	**Shadowfax (Binghamton, N.Y.) and Dama, Toucan and Crow (Greenfield, Vt.)**
Ordering Cycle	**Every 4 to 6 Weeks**

Eight people began this co-op in the fall of 1973. Steve Hoag describes some of the Mountain Co-op's operations:

"We order food every 4–6 weeks. The managers are responsible for changing the list every month, based on demand and whim. The order list was up to 50 items at first, gradually diminishing to 30–40 items. Recently, we reorganized and the list is now up to 70 items. Any member can actually order anything that the distributor has to offer if that member buys at least the distributor's minimum amount."

Mountain Co-op has grown to about seventy families, which are divided into four teams. Every operation is done separately except the shopping and distribution. Here's how Steve describes the average buying cycle:

"Four managers call a meeting (sometimes a collator and bookkeeper are included) to decide on the list of foods and the newsletter.

—List is sent to secretaries for typing and printing

—Orders are sent by mail to members

—Members write what they want plus cost and send order and money to one of the collators

—Collating group tallies up all orders and decides what to order from distributor based on demand

—Collator calls in order to distributor

—Distributor delivers order to House of the Month

—Breakdown occurs usually on a Thursday or Friday

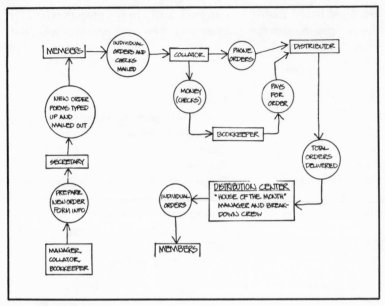

Mountain Co-op
East Stroudsburg, Pennsylvania

—Pick-up occurs Saturday afternoon between 1 and 5

All are volunteers at this point. Within each group, specific jobs are decided by that group . . . New members are assessed $5 . . . We are trying a new thing for new members—meetings with managers before they join to get them and us acquainted."

Steve reports that a Children's Preschool Co-op grew out of the food co-op, and is now a separate entity. Potluck suppers have also been held. His advice to new groups:

"Wholesalers can't alway supply what you want—ordering from several distributors can alleviate this. Members expect to get everything they order; this is just about impossible.

—Be careful to check everything you get from distributor

—When starting a co-op, get advice, but essentially do what you feel intuitively is best to do—don't necessarily model yourself after another co-op

—Volunteer work is most efficient

—Don't try to do too much at one time—go slow—see what you are able to accomplish easily, then grow from there."

Name	**R Co-op**
Location	**Emmaus, Pennsylvania**
Money System	**Preorder/Pay-on-Delivery (Modified Storefront)**
Distribution System	**Around-the-Room**
Work System	**Teams**
Types of Foods	**Dried Goods, Produce, Some Meats**
Sources of Foods	**Shadowfax (Binghamton, N.Y.), Local Farmers and Livestock Producers**
Ordering Cycle	**Every Two Weeks**

I've included this example because often people working together can provide the perfect group to begin a food co-op. The R Co-op is composed of members of the Rodale Press publishing company in rural southeastern Pennsylvania. The R Co-op took the form, from the beginning, of a modified storefront, but that was partly because they received strong commitments from interested people from the beginning, and partly because the company for whom they work was sympathetic to the plan and donated an empty office for them to use.

Ray Wolf, a staff editor at Rodale Press, explained how the co-op began:

"Our group got together at work, and decided to try and get a co-op off the ground. We had about three formal meetings, and many of those famous hallway conversations about the problems and advantages of a co-op. I went to two area co-ops and talked to their people about problems encountered, as well as talking to people at work who had experiences with other co-ops. We finally got things together and had notices passed out with pay checks telling people what we wanted to do, and making preference lists available to get an idea of what everyone would be interested in buying. From this list we worked up our first order. All of our foods have long storage life, as we have no refrigeration available. I should point out that we did not want to set up a buying club. We decided to make the commitment and go big, so we stocked an inventory of goods. We got lucky and attended a bankruptcy auction of a local natural foods store and for $150 we picked up over $600 worth of goodies. Backtracking a little, we charged members a ten-dollar joining fee to give us operating capital. After the auction, we spent most of the rest of the money on an order of rice, wheat, corn, rye, nuts, dried fruits, cereals, etc., leaving about $60 to set up . . . we currently have 52 members."

R Co-op has benefited greatly from the interest shown by the company its members work for. Part of their produce and cheese order, for instance, is combined with the order used by the kitchen staff in the company's lunchroom. They have no rent or overhead to speak of, and only have to cover waste or spoilage.

Ray's advice to new co-ops in the early stages: "Keep it simple."

NOTE: I decided against presenting a flow chart for R Co-op because the activity is an ongoing process, day after day. Members see each other at work, and so money is paid whenever they have the chance, new order forms are made available there, and the food is picked up from the spare office lent to them by the company. The system used is basically the standard preorder/pay-on-delivery system, except that the food is stored in a room, and the orders compiled as members get there on certain days after work.

Name	**Park Forest Food Co-op**
Location	**Park Forest, Illinois**
Money System	**Preorder/Pay-on-Delivery**
Distribution System	**Teams**
Work System	**Regular and Rotating plus Pay-the-Broker**
Types of Foods	**Meats, Produce, Eggs, Cheeses, Dried Goods**
Sources of Foods	**S. Water Street Terminal Market (Chicago) and Local Distributors of Other Products**
Ordering Cycle	**Weekly**

This co-op grew, by choice, from a handful of people to more than two hundred and fifty in about one year. They hired a manager who shops and runs the finances, and expanded their order form to include much more than the original produce selections. Park Forest now does its distribution from the back of a laundromat. Susan Youngdahl lists this as an average weekly cycle:

"Monday & Tuesday—callers call members for orders

Wednesday—individual orders are tabulated and orders for items that must be placed in advance of pick-up (such as cheese) are phoned in

Friday, 2:00 A.M.—truck leaves for S. Water Street Market where produce and other items are purchased; truck returns to Park Forest about 8:30 A.M.; truck is unloaded and then goes to local eggery. At the distribution center, produce is weighed and cheese is cut. Individual orders are then bagged. The center opens for pick-up at 3:00 P.M."

Susan advises: "A group should be prepared to deal with the problem of extra produce (e.g., the co-op has orders for ¾ case—what to do with the extra ¼), or orders not picked up, or only produce of poor quality available . . . People starting a co-op should set some policies about these things before operation starts."

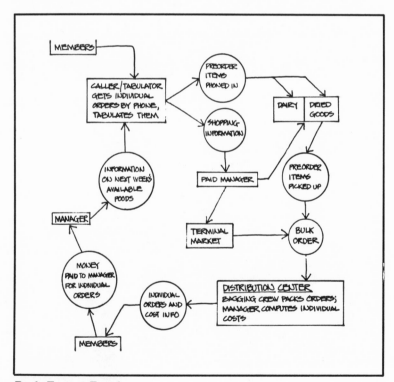

**Park Forest Food
Park Forest, Illinois**

Name	**Ozark Food Co-op**
Location	**Fayetteville, Arkansas**
Money System	**Preorder/Prepaid**
Distribution System	**Teams**
Work System	**Regular and Rotating Jobs**
Types of Foods	**Dried Goods (an Extensive List), Herbs, Spices**
	Some Produce
Sources of Foods	**Iowa City Warehouse, National Distributors of Natural Foods, Local Farmers**
Ordering Cycle	**Monthly**

This co-op started in 1971 as a small buying-club-type operation, "moving from different members' houses into the back of a bicycle shop," writes Kelley, one of its prime movers now

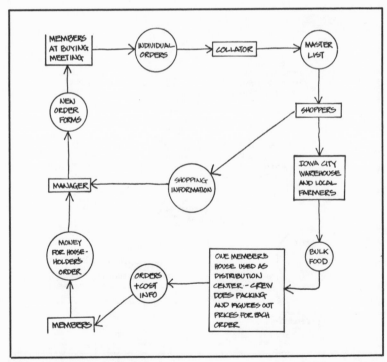

Ozark Food Co-op
Fayetteville, Arkansas

that it serves about five hundred members out of a permanent storefront.

I have included this co-op because it is not at all close to many first-hand sources of supply, but has grown to provide a wide range of selections simply on the strength of the size of its membership. The flow chart that accompanies this description represents its original, small co-op cycle of buying.

Kelley's advice to new small co-ops is "Shop around! Wholesalers usually aren't willing to give you the best price right away, of course. Ask co-ops or friendly stores for good sources. Of course, the bigger orders you buy, the more likely you are to get better discounts."

The Ozark Food Co-op has grown into a several-service operation, with one particular aspect providing the setting for one of Kelley's favorite incidents. Along with milling flour, baking bread, offering nonfood items like shampoos, soaps, and natural-bristle tooth and hair brushes, Ozark also produces its own natural peanut butter. He writes that "the peanut butter machine wasn't grounded for a while, and it gave our barefoot grinders a slight shock!"

Keep your feet on the ground, whatever you do!

Name	**House of Kuumba**
Location	**New York City**
Money System	**Preorder/Pay-on-Delivery**
Distribution System	**Around-the-Room**
Work System	**Regular and Rotating Jobs**
Types of Foods	**Produce, Eggs, Cheeses, Bread, Frozen Fish**
Sources of Foods	**Hunt's Point Terminal Market (New York City), Regional Farmers, Regional Distributors**
Ordering Cycle	**Weekly**

The House of Kuumba Co-op's coordinator, Joe James, explained that it is "an outgrowth of a cultural center, and an attempt to strengthen roots in the community . . . members provide each other with skills and services through the co-op." The black cultural arts group initiated their co-op in August of 1973, and averages about twenty orders each week.

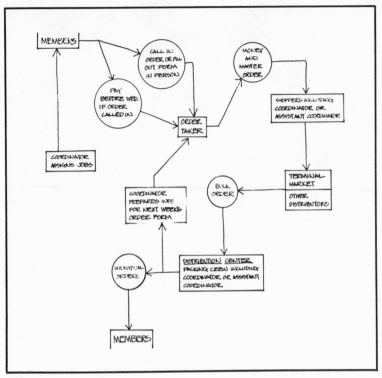

**House of Kuumba
New York City**

"At first, distribution occurred in the loft theater of the sponsoring group, and later moved to its present site, Synod House, St. John's Cathedral," he continued. "Family units are required to have completed ½ work unit (approximately one hour) before each buy. The coordinator and the assistant coordinator are responsible for seeing that the co-op functions."

Joe stated that "as the co-op's treasury expanded, we exempted 'reliable' members from having to bring cash until they picked up their food." As the flow chart indicates, household orders are placed by telephone. A $10 membership fee is charged.

"Volume commands quality and better prices," Joe adds, advising new groups to "find people with a need, time, understanding of how co-op systems work, and a common ideological or other unifying background."

Name	**107th St. Block, Broadway Local Food Co-op**
Location	**New York City's Upper West Side**
Money System	**Preorder/Prepaid/Credits**
Distribution System	**Category Lists**
Work System	**Everybody-Works- Every- Week**
Types of Foods	**Produce, Meats, Eggs, Cheeses, Other Dairy Products, Dried Goods, Breads**
Sources of Foods	**Hunt's Point Terminal Market (New York City), Regional Distributors, Regional Farmers**
Ordering Cycle	**Weekly**

The Broadway Local is made up of twelve small groups of people who live in different neighborhoods of New York City's Upper West Side. The Local is not a federation of small co-ops, but rather one co-op that began five years ago with twelve people, and grew and grew and grew. I was one of the original twelve, and have seen it divide into two groups, then three, then six and now up to twelve.

My branch, or block, of the Local, is 107th Street. Each block may conduct its internal block organization any way it chooses. I'm including our block in this section because it could easily function separately if there were no eleven other blocks. If you'll note on the flow chart, there is a person whose job it is to transport the block's money and master list to the people doing the shopping that week (someone in another block most of the time, since the big jobs like shopping and master book-keeping are rotated among all twelve blocks). Two or three more people are in charge of picking up the block's food order and transporting it to where we do our breakdown, a lobby of an apartment building. These four people would become shop-pers if the block were operating on its own, and everything else would remain the same.

Here's how our block operates: Each Monday evening at 7:30 P.M., members come to a specific apartment for a short meeting. New order forms are there. Meetings are held in the same apartment each week, to make it easier for people who do not order every week. The block coordinator at the meeting asks for volunteers for the jobs for that week, or else makes

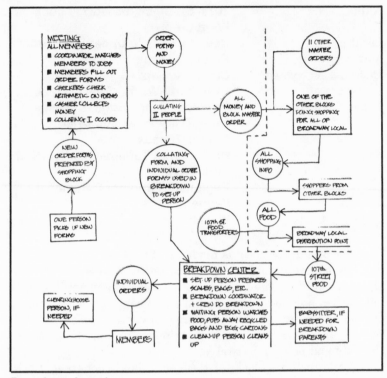

Broadway Local
West 107th Street Block
New York City

suggestions to some people as to the jobs they might be able to fill. After the meeting, where policy matters, complaints and changes of procedure are discussed, members fill out an order form, take it to one of the three people checking arithmetic, then to the cashier, who collects money, and finally to the person doing Collating I. At the end of the meeting, the half-finished collating sheet, the individual order forms and the money are given to the people doing Collating II, or the bookkeeping/accounting/totaling part. Collating I simply involves the transfer of the information from the individual order forms to the big collating form.

Collators compile the master shopping list for the block, and it, together with the money, gets picked up Tuesday evening at 6 P.M. and taken to the block that's doing the shopping. The individual order forms and the large collating form are delivered to the Set-Up person. Thursday afternoon at 3 P.M. the Set-Up person, who has the individual order forms and the large collating form, goes to the lobby of the apartment building used as our distribution center. In a closet off the lobby is the "Co-op wagon," an old bureau mounted on wheels which contains all the large and small bags, waxed paper, cutting knife, scales, egg carton, pencils, marking pens, stapler, scissors, tape and anything else deemed necessary for distribution. The Set-Up person wheels out the wagon, taking also the broom and dustpan, and locks the closet. Individual order forms, which have been marked with big numbers, are stapled to the large-size grocery bags, and placed around the room. Scales are put in place. At 3:20, the food transporters begin carting our block's food from the central distribution point fourteen blocks away, using either a member's car or the Local truck. The Set-Up person sees that the food is unloaded properly; the collating form is cut into strips, and these are turned over, along with the closet key, to the Breakdown Coordinator at 3:50 P.M. At 4 P.M., the Breakdown Crew arrives, and the breakdown is done for the next hour. From 5 P.M. to 6:15 P.M., members may pick up their food. During that time, someone stays with the food to be certain there are no mistakes or thefts. That person also receives egg cartons and bags from members when they come for their food, and puts them in the proper drawer in the wagon. A Clean-Up person arrives and does the sweeping and disposal of cartons and boxes between 5:30 P.M. and 6 P.M. When the Coordinator arrives, the key is turned over to him or her. The Clearinghouse person gets her food near the end of the allotted period, and takes with her the sheet which recorded shortages and missing items, to make her work easier. Sunday afternoon one member picks up the new order forms from the Local storefront and the process begins again Monday night.

Appendix B
Glossary

Agribusiness the term used to describe corporations involved in huge farming operations distinguished by chemical production methods and domination of the food production and delivery systems.

Back order procedure used in some co-ops which use warehouses as a source of supply; a member co-op places an order for a wholesale amount of some food item, and the warehouse keeps the order on file until that item comes in, at which time the co-op is notified.

Bagger someone who works on the dividing up of the co-op's food order into each household's order.

Basket wicker-type container of various sizes used for wholesale food sales.

Bookkeeper same as treasurer.

Breakdown a term used for dividing up the co-op's total food order into each household's order.

Broker someone whose job (full-time) it is to arrange for the purchase of bulk quantities of foods by institutions, supermarkets or co-ops, and who is paid either a commission or a fee or both for this service.

Bulk large wholesale quantity; often used to designate a several-case minimum order.

Bushel a measure of volume (2150.42 cubic inches) used in wholesale food distribution to indicate the space a container contains.

Buyer on the co-op level, someone who does the purchasing, and may choose from several selections, such as at the wholesale produce market, or may pick up an order that has been previously placed by the co-op with a distributor.

Buying Club commonly used term for a small co-op.

Caller person who does the same volunteer job as an order-taker, but always does it by telephone.

Carton heavy cardboard box used for shipping and selling foods in various wholesale distribution quantities.

Cashier possible term for person in the co-op who collects money from members; at the wholesale market, the person who is paid for wholesale produce after it has been purchased, and who may validate the slip of paper authorizing the release of that produce for delivery by the loading foreman to the co-op's vehicle.

Cell Pack term used for individual cellophane-bag packaging units, usually one-pound quantities of carrots.

Clearinghouse device used to match misplaced food found in one household's bags with another household erroneously shorted that same food; one person may volunteer to act as the co-op's clearinghouse, taking phone calls and matching information.

Collator a possible term for the person who combines all the household orders into one master shopping list, and may check, in a preorder-prepaid system, whether the total money received equals the amount of money needed to purchase the total number of food items ordered; may also be called the tabulator or the tallier.

Co-op a group of people who agree to pool their buying power for certain items, arrange to purchase them wholesale, and share the tasks involved in carrying out this procedure, in which the extra time spent is compensated by the extra money saved.

Coordinator term for the person who oversees all stages during a particular buying cycle. The coordinator may match members to volunteer jobs, may keep work records, may assign jobs, may be expected to fill in for members who cannot do their job, may be responsible for making or helping to make decisions if the regular routine is disrupted for any reason.

Coupon Exchange a system of making available to people who can use them any printed discount coupons one would usually throw away. No obligation is laid down that one must be left if one is taken.

Crate wholesale food container usually made from thin wooden slats, bound by wire.

Credit term used for the subtracting of an amount of money from the total owed equal to an amount previously paid for which no food was received; used in the preorder-prepaid-credits system instead of refunding cash; also, offered by some wholesale distributors when a co-op has received a quantity of poor quality or wrong food.

Deposit token amount of money paid by a co-op member when joining the group; used for expenses, or, in preorder/pay-on-delivery system, to pay for first week's food; may also be used in pay-on-delivery system as added incentive for members to pick up food on time; may be required by some wholesale distributors from whom preorder items are purchased.

Direct Charge a system, at present more popular in Canada than in the United States, in which the co-op's operating expenses for the month are divided equally by all adult members, and in which the cost of the food is exactly the price paid to the wholesaler.

Dispatcher same as seller at wholesale produce market.

Distribution on the co-op level, the system used for dividing up the co-op's total food order into each household's order; on the wholesale level, the process of selling bulk wholesale food items.

Distribution Center the particular space the co-op uses for dividing up the total food order into each household's order; payment and/or ordering next week's food may also take place here if the co-op's system has decided to do so.

Distributor term for the company or person who sells wholesale quantities of different kinds of foods.

Dry Goods term for unprocessed, packaged or natural foods, including beans, rices, flours, all other grains, seeds, nuts, cereals, pastas, honey, oils, teas, bottled goods, dried fruits, herbs, peanut butter, etc.

Federating the process of joining together several small independent food co-ops in a loose mutually beneficial alliance. Does not mean all operations, responsibilities, sources, or costs will be combined or shared.

Film Bag term used for heavy plastic bags.

Flat Carton container, similar in materials to a regular carton, but shallower, usually with a lid-type top instead of a full-cover top.

Flat Tray container similar to a flat carton, but usually even more shallow.

Grades, U.S. government standard ratings, either voluntary or mandatory, placed on some foods. To obtain more information, see Appendix E.

Household term used to describe the people who fill out one order; may be one individual, two people living together, a family, a few families or a few people living together or simply buying their food together.

Leftovers the food remaining after every household order has been filled; the result when almost enough to equal a bulk quantity is ordered by co-op members and the bulk quantity is purchased; also called surplus.

Loading Foreman at the wholesale produce market, the person in charge of actually delivering the bulk quantity of food that has been ordered and paid for; loading foreman generally instructs members of the loading crew to execute the order, loading it into the co-op's shopping vehicle; may also serve as cashier for the distributor.

Manager possible term for a person paid by the co-op to do its buying (see Broker); possible term for coordinator.

Markup the amount of money, either in dollars and cents, or in the form of a percentage of the total dollar amount of food ordered, or a surcharge, that the co-op regularly charges members to cover operating expenses and to provide a slight financial cushion to cover small unexpected price rises.

Master List also called master shopping list, it refers to the compiled totals of each food item that shoppers use to purchase the wholesale order; the end product of the process called tabulating or collating.

Natural Foods foods presented to the consumer that are free of preservatives of any kind.

Newsletter device used by some co-ops regularly to inform members of current policy, meeting and work schedules, introductions to and of new members, or to share recipes and other useful information.

Open Case Lots same as split cases.

Order Form the sheet used by a member, listing the foods available and sometimes the prices, to place an order.

Order-Form Maker the person whose volunteer job it is to prepare new order forms for the upcoming shopping cycle and make them available to the members at the meeting or through whatever system the co-op uses.

Orders on the co-op level, the household's total requested amount of food; at the wholesale level, the co-op's total requested bulk amount of food.

Order Taker the person in the co-op who collects each individual household's order, and passes on this collected information to the tabulator, the coordinator or the shopper; the order taker may gather this information by telephone.

Organic term used to describe foods grown or produced with no pesticides, herbicides, fungicides, fertilizers, or chemicals of any kind and presented to the consumer with no preservatives of any kind added.

Packing the process of dividing up the co-op's total order into each household's food order; also called bagging or doing breakdown; done by the packing crew.

Pay-On-Delivery a type of system used by co-ops in which members order food in advance and pay for it when it is received by the members.

Pickup Point the place where members get their individual food order; same as distribution center.

Potluck one system of operation in which each member puts in a set amount of money, and the total amount is used to purchase a bulk quantity of some foods at the discretion of the shopper; the food is then equally divided among all the members.

Preorder on the co-op level, the term used to describe the process of members listing their exact food preferences before the co-op shopping is done; on the wholesale level, the process used to inform certain distributors of the co-op's exact bulk order desired, which is then picked up or delivered.

Prepaid term used to describe advancing the money for a household's food order before the food is received.

Produce fresh agricultural products, usually fruits and vegetables.

Producer person or company which grows or develops foods, either through farming, the raising of animals, fowl or fish, or other process, such as making available honey or maple syrup.

Purveyor person or company selling foods wholesale.

Scales devices used to measure and weigh out bulk foods that are sold wholesale by the pound.

Secretary possible term for the person who prepares new order forms or records volunteer work assignments or minutes of meetings.

Seller person at wholesale produce market who accepts orders for bulk quantities of the food his company sells; usually issues a voucher or ticket with which the buyer actually pays for and receives the food.

Shopper one of the persons who goes to the wholesale market to buy the co-op's food order and may also pick up preordered foods.

Shortages the result when less food than the total co-op's order is purchased or received; usually caused by insufficient quantities being available from the wholesale distributor or when the co-op's order does not equal a full bulk quantity.

Split Cases practice of a few wholesalers in which part of a bulk quantity is added to the regular bulk quantity to make up a co-op's exact desired order, requiring the wholesaler to open a case, carton, or crate to add the extra number of items.

Stall facility at a wholesale market from which the distributor or purveyor sells food.

Storefront type of large co-op operation in which members collectively run a store, including a small paid staff (perhaps even one person), and at which members may purchase stocked foods at wholesale prices; this type of operation is only viable for very large co-ops or for a federation of co-ops; the term can also refer to a kind of urban building once used as a store, but now available for community use.

Supplier person or company which distributes food wholesale.

Surcharge one method used by co-ops to raise the money needed to pay operating expenses in which a set amount of money or a set percentage of the total is added to each household's food bill.

Surplus Food same as leftovers.

Tabulator a possible term for the person who combines all the household orders into one master shopping list, and may check, in a preorder-prepaid system, whether the total money received equals the amount of money needed to purchase the total number of food items ordered; may also be called the collator.

Tallier person who tallies or adds up individual orders; see Collator or Tabulator.

Terminal Market the wholesale produce-selling district of any metropolitan area where distributors sell bulk quantities of foods; so named because it's where food shipped from outside the immediate region ends up for sale.

Ticket receipt given by the seller at the wholesale market to the buyer which is used to verify the purchase; also called a voucher.

Treasurer possible term for the person who volunteers to collect the money for each household's order; person may also collect new member's initial deposit, record refundable membership fees, compute individual food prices, co-sign checks, or keep financial records for tax or other purposes; may also be called bookkeeper.

Vendor same as distributor; usually applies to distributors at the wholesale produce market.

Voucher same as ticket.

Warehousing the process of several co-ops combining their projected order of some items, purchasing these items in large bulk quantity, and storing them in a jointly run facility; on the small co-op level, buying an extra amount of non-perishable food when a good price is available, and storing it until the next shopping cycle.

Wholesale term used when foods are sold by the producer or distributor rather than by a retailer or merchant, resulting in a savings because the retailer's overhead, expenses, and profits are eliminated.

Appendix C
Food Grades and Standards

Federal food standards are often mistakenly thought to be indicators of high quality or high nutritional content alone, and it is important for food co-op members to understand when to look for graded evaluations on foods and when to overlook them. In buying foods wholesale for the first time, there may be an inclination to overvalue grade labelings on some products and to worry about their absence when dealing directly with farmers. This inclination should be overcome at the outset.

To begin with, there are mandatory and voluntary standards. Mandatory standards set by the U.S. Department of Agriculture apply for the most part, to minimum content requirements in meat products, such as beef stew or chopped ham. The Food and Drug Administration (FDA) provides for standards of identity (establishing by its content what it is and how it may be labeled), standards of minimum quality (canned fruits and vegetables judged for tenderness, color, and freedom from defects) and standards of fill of container, to insure a certain weight for certain packages.

Voluntary standards of the USDA, not required by law, have been created for beef, veal and calf, lamb and mutton; poultry, including turkey, chicken, duck, goose, guinea hen, and squab; eggs; manufactured dairy products, including butter, Cheddar cheese and instant nonfat dry milk; fresh fruit and vegetables and nuts; canned, frozen, and dried fruits and vegetables and related products; rice, dry beans, peas, and unprocessed grain.

Grade standards for beef, veal and calf, and lamb and mutton are determined by color, firmness, texture, and degree of marbling. In poultry, the proportion of edible meat to bone, the "finish" of the bird, and freedom from defects are used as criteria.

Eggs are judged by weight, appearance, and adjudged suitability to various methods of cooking. Butter standards relate to eating quality, based on flavor, texture, and body. Cheddar cheese grades are also influenced by age or degree of cure. Instant nonfat dry milk standards stem from flavor, color uniformity, bacterial count, dispersibility, solubility index, and moisture and milkfat content.

Fresh and processed fruits and vegetables are to be judged for color, shape, size, maturity, and number and degree of defects. Processed foods also include flavor and tenderness in their grading.

Rice and dry beans and peas measure uniform shape, size, color, moisture content, damage, and foreign material.

Now that you feel all these factors have been taken into account and are reflected in the grade listing, note these facts:

—Inspection for grading is mainly done visually.

—Processors, distributors, packers or others seeking USDA official grading services must pay a fee to receive them.

—Butter's grades are B, A, and AA, while beef includes eight different grades.

—Rice may be graded from U.S.1 to U.S.6, while instant nonfat dry milk has only one grade, U.S. Extra.

—On page 8 of *USDA Grade Standards for Food— How They Are Developed and Used* (USDA—PA 1027, August, 1974—stock # 0100–03326), the following is stated: "For most commodities, if an official U.S. grade name or grade shield is used, however, the product must have been officially graded or inspected. *The only exceptions are for fresh fruits, vegetables, and a few other products, where the practice of grade labeling without official inspection has existed through the years.*"

State and local governments may institute their own grades or standards also, and the FDA advises state and local governments on public health and sanitation standards.

If the co-op would like the complete, official government rundown on grades and standards, write the USDA (see Appendix E) or the state Department of Agriculture. Organizations with information analyzing or criticizing this set of procedures includes the Agribusiness Accountability Project, c/o Center for Community Change, 1000 Wisconsin NW, Washington, D.C. 20007; Rodale Press, Emmaus, Pennsylvania 18049; the Ralph Nader series of studies on food-related topics available from the Center for the Study of Responsive Law, P.O. Box 19367, Washington, D.C. 20036; Consumer Action, Now, 30 East 68th Street, New York City, N.Y.; and many city or regional departments of consumer affairs offices.

Appendix D
Regional Sources of Information about Neighborhood Co-ops and Sources of Supply

You will not find a list of all known co-ops in the United States in this book because it is impossible to tabulate and keep up-to-date. Each regional contact has a far better chance of presenting you and your group with an accurate, current listing than anyone else. Co-ops often change their location, method of operation, membership rules, and sometimes even their name. The regional contacts listed here are the most stable, least likely to change their vital information, and most able to put you in contact with other co-ops in your area.

Regional food co-op contacts will also be excellent sources of wholesale produce markets. When writing to them for other information, ask additionally if they know of markets other than those listed below.

This list is prepared in zip code order. When none was available, an entry is placed in closest order. If you find the listing for the wholesale food market closest to you, and you know where the address is located, you can visit there with no trouble; if you are unsure of how to get there, send a postcard, addressed to "Director, Market," or "Market Manager," and the market's address, asking for directions to get to the market from where you live.

If no market is listed in your immediate area, see if one is listed in a nearby area. To learn whether there is one closer to you, send a postcard to the Marketing Director, Department of

Agriculture, c/o your state capital. Some of these addresses are listed below.

Many locales have farmers' markets. Some are listed below. To learn of others, check with your closest Department of Agriculture office, state Department of Consumer Affairs, regional farmers, or newspaper or television news desks or food editors.

New England

NEFCO
Don Lubin
8 Ashford Street
Allston, Massachusetts
02134
(617) A-LIVING

New York City

Direct Supply
3803 Cannon Place
Bronx, New York 10463

New York State

Clear Eye Warehouse
367 Orchard
Rochester, New York 14606
(716) 235-1080

Philadelphia & Area

Philadelphia Federation of Food Co-ops
3300 Race Street
Philadelphia, Pennsylvania 19104

Washington D.C. & Area

Community Warehouse
2010 Kendall St. NE
Washington, D.C. 20002
(202) 832-4517

Florida

Sunshine Co-operative Association
4435 N.W. Second
Miami, Florida 33127

Kentucky

Good Foods Co-op
314½ South Ashland
Lexington, Kentucky 40502

Ohio

Common Market Warehouse
Box 8253
Columbus, Ohio 43201
(614) 294-0145

Michigan

Michigan Federation of Food Co-ops
411 Jackson
Ann Arbor, Michigan 48103
(313) 761-4642

Iowa

BLOOMING PRAIRIE WAREHOUSE
529 South Gilbert
Iowa City, Iowa 52240
(319) 338-5300

Wisconsin

Intra-Community
  Co-operative
1335 Gilson
Madison, Wisconsin 53715
(608) 251-2403

Minnesota & Area

SCOOP/People's Warehouse
123 East 26th
Minneapolis, Minnesota
  55404
(612) 824-2634

Chicago & Area

FOOD CO-OP PROJECT
64 East Lake Street
Chicago, Illinois 60601
(312) 269-8101

St. Louis & Area

MCCA Warehouse
4140 West Pine
St. Louis, Missouri 63130

Kansas City & Area

Kansas City Grain
  Warehouse
4109 Locust
Kansas City, Missouri 64110
(816) 561-6301

Dallas & Area

Co-operation
5423 Druid Lane
Dallas, Texas 75209

Austin & Area

Austin Community Project
1602 West 12th
Austin, Texas 78703
(512) 477-6255

Colorado

Common Market of Colorado
1100 Champa
Denver, Colorado 80204
(303) 893-3430

Arizona, New Mexico

People's Warehouse
411 North 7th
Tucson, Arizona 85705
(602) 884-9951

Southern California

Southern California Co-
  operating Community
11615 Mississippi
Los Angeles, California
90025
(213) 478-1922

Northern California

San Francisco Warehouse
1559 Bancroft
San Francisco, California
94124
(415) 822-8830

Hawaii

Kokua Country Foods
2357 South Beretania
Honolulu, Hawaii 96814
(808) 941-1922

Oregon

Starflower
385 Lawrence
Eugene, Oregon 97401

Washington

Co-operating Communities
4030 22nd Avenue West
Seattle, Washington 98199
(206) 283-3777

Massachusetts

New England Produce
 Center
Chelsea, MA 02150

Boston Market Terminal
Market Street
Everett, MA 02149

Director of Markets
Department of Agriculture
100 Cambridge Street
Boston, MA 02202

Farmers' Market
Haymarket Square
Boston MA

Maine

Department of Agriculture
State Office Building
Division of Agricultural
 Promotion
Augusta, ME 04330

Farmers' Market
Bangor, ME

Farmers' Market
Rockport, ME

Connecticut

Executive Secretary
Connecticut Marketing
 Authority
101 Reserve Road
Hartford, CT 06114

New Haven Food Terminal
New Haven, CT 06511

Farmers' Market
Bridgeport, CT

New Jersey

Gloucester County Agri.
 Coop. Association
Box 156 — Market Place
Glassboro, NJ 08028

Hammonton Coop. Fruit
 Auction Association
Box 185
Hammonton, NJ 08037

Tri-County Coop. Auction
 Market
Box 185
Highstown, NJ 08520

Farmers' Market
Elizabethtown, NJ

Produce Terminal Market
Vineland, NJ   .

Newark Terminal Market
Chapel Street and Albert
 Avenue
Newark, NJ

New York

Bronx Terminal Market
151st Street and Cromwell
 Avenue
Bronx, NY 10451

Hunt's Point Terminal
Market
Bronx, NY 10474

Brooklyn Terminal Market
Co-op
83rd Street and Foster
Avenue
Brooklyn, NY

Brooklyn Provisions Market
North Sixth Street
Brooklyn, NY

Delancey Street Market
Delancey Street
New York City, NY

Capital District Coop
Menands Market
Albany, NY 12204

Central N.Y. Regional
Market
2100 Park Street
Syracuse, NY 13208

Utica Regional Market
Nine Wurz Avenue
Utica, NY 13501

Niagara Frontier Growers
Coop. Market
1400–1500 Clinton Street
Buffalo, NY 14206

Rochester Public Market
280 North Union Street
Rochester, NY 14605

Genesee Valley Regional
Market
900 Jefferson Road
Rochester, NY 14625

Farmers' Market
Bethpage, Long Island, NY

Pennsylvania

Produce Market
100 19th Street
Pittsburgh, PA 15222

Northern Ohio Food
Terminal
Rt. 1, Box 123
Clarion, PA 16214

Farmer's Market
Public Square
Wilkes-Barre, Pa.

Farmers' Market
Town Common
Bradford, PA

Farmers' Market
Fairgrounds
Allentown, PA

Food Distribution Center
300 S. Galloway Street
Philadelphia, PA 19148

Farmers' Market
Reading Terminal
Philadelphia, PA

Maryland

U.S. Department of
Agriculture
Agricultural Research
Center
East Building 307
Beltsville, MD 20705

U.S. Department of
Agriculture
Head License Section, F. &
V. Division
10414 Royal Road
Silver Springs, MD 20903

Greater Baltimore
Consolidated   Wholesale
Food Market
1115 One Charles Center
Baltimore, MD 21201

Virginia

Director, Division of
Markets
203 North Government
Street
Room 407 C
Richmond, VA 23219

Farmers' Market
Virginia Beach, VA

North Carolina

State Farmers' Market
1301 Hodges Street
Raleigh, NC 27604

Produce Terminal
Charlotte, NC

South Carolina

Columbia State Farmers'
Market
Box 13506
Columbia, SC 29201

Horry County Farmers'
Market
Box 428
Loris, SC 29569

Greenville Farmers'
Wholesale Market
Camp Road
Greenville, SC 29609

Farmers' Market
Charleston, SC

Georgia

State Farmers' Market
Forest Park
Atlanta, GA 30050

State Farmers' Market
Augusta, GA 30901

State Farmers' Market
Cairo, GA 31728

State Farmers' Market
Thomasville, GA 31792

State Farmers' Market
318 Tenth Avenue
Columbus, GA 31903

Florida

State Farmers' Market
Box 216
Palatka, FL 32077

State Farmers' Market
Box 98
Starke, FL 32091

Jacksonville Produce
Market
1780 West Beaver Street
Jacksonville, FL 32209

Gadsden County State
Farmers' Market
Box 384
Quincy, FL 32351

State Farmers' Market
Box 696
Bonifay, FL 32425

State Farmers' Market
Box 908
Sanford, FL 32771

State Farmers' Market
Box 3278
Florida City, FL 33030

State Farmers' Market
Pompano Beach, FL 33060

Food Terminal Market
Miami, FL 33156

State Farmers' Market
Box 866
Fort Pierce, FL 33450

State Farmers' Market
Box 637
Plant City, FL 33566

Tampa Wholesale Produce
Market
2801 Hillsborough Avenue
Box 11027
Tampa, FL 33610

State Farmers' Market
Box 425
Wauchula, FL 33873

State Farmers' Market
Box 187
Fort Myers, FL 33902

State Farmers' Market
420 New Market Road
Immokalee, FL 33934

Alabama

Director, Marketing Division
Alabama Department of
Agriculture
Box 3336
Montgomery, AL 36109

Wiregrass Farmers' Produce
Market
Box 309 — Old Cowarts
Road
Dothan, AL 36301

Farmers' Market
Birmingham, AL

Kentucky

Louisville Produce Terminal
4601 Jennings Lane
Louisville, KY 40218

Ohio

Produce Terminal
4561 East Fifth Avenue
Columbus, OH 43219

Northern Ohio Food
Terminal
3800 Orange Avenue
Cleveland, OH 44115

Produce Terminal Market
1700 Hubbard Road
Youngstown, OH 44502

Produce Terminal
Produce Drive
Cincinnati, OH 45202

Indiana

Indianapolis Produce
Terminal
Indianapolis, IN 46204

Produce Terminal Market
Vincennes, IN 47591

Michigan

Gratiot Central Market
Gratiot and Fisher
Detroit, MI

Detroit Union Produce
  Terminal
7200 West Fort Street and
  Green Street
Detroit, MI 48209

Lansing City Market
333 North Cedar Street
Lansing, MI 48910

Benton Harbor Fruit Market
Box 148
Benton Harbor, MI 49022

Grand Rapids Food Market
  Authority
1030 North Terminal
  Crescent
Grand Rapids, MI 49534

Iowa

Produce Terminal Market
Des Moines, IA

Farmers' Market
Cedar Rapids, IA

Wisconsin

Produce Terminal Market
300 N. Broadway
Milwaukee, WI 53202

Produce Terminal Market
Stevens Point, WI 54481

Produce Terminal Market
Antigo, WI 54409

Produce Terminal Market
Plover, WI 54467

North Dakota

Wholesale Food Market
Grafton, ND 58237

Wholesale Food Market
Hoople, ND 58243

Montana

Produce Terminal
Billings, MT

Wholesale Food Market
Missoula, MT

Illinois

South Water Market
Chicago, IL 60608

Produce Terminal
Rock Island, IL

Missouri

Produce Terminal Market
Joplin, MO

St. Louis Produce Market
Produce Row
St. Louis, MO 63102

Produce Terminal Market
50 East Fifth Street
Kansas City, MO 64106

Kansas

Produce Terminal Market
Wichita, KA

Nebraska

Hastings Farmers' Market
Hastings, NB

Louisiana

French Market
424 Barracks Street
New Orleans, LA 70116

Department of Agriculture
Box 4052, Capitol Station
Baton Rouge, LA 70804

Oklahoma

Farmers' Market
Oklahoma City, OK

Texas

Area Supervisor—Market-
ing
Department of Agriculture
4619 Insurance Lane,
Suite 202
Dallas, TX 75205

Houston Produce Center
3100 Produce Row
Houston, TX 77023

San Antonio Produce
Terminal Market
1500 South Zarzamore
Street
San Antonio, TX 78207

Farmers' Market
San Antonio, TX 78285

Director of Marketing
Texas Dept. of Agriculture
Box 12874, Capitol Station,
Austin, TX 78753

Colorado

Produce Terminal Market
2400 Lorimor Street
Denver, CO 80205

Wholesale Food Market
Pueblo, CO

Utah

Farmers' Market
Salt Lake City, UT

Arizona

Farmers' Market
Tucson, AZ

Produce Terminal Market
Nogales, AZ

Wholesale Produce Market
Phoenix, AZ

New Mexico

Wholesale Produce Center
Mesquite, NM

California

City Market of Los Angeles
1050 South San Pedro Street
Los Angeles, CA 90015

Los Angeles Union Terminal
746 South Central Avenue
Los Angeles, CA 90706

Golden Gate Produce
Terminal
Terminal Court
San Francisco, CA 94080

Wholesale Food Market
Oxnard, CA 93030

Wholesale Food Market
Fresno, CA

Produce Terminal Market
Walla Walla, WA 99362

Oregon

Terminal Market
2300 South Commercial
    Street
Salem, OR 97302

Wholesale Produce Market
Portland, OR

Washington

Produce Terminal Market
West Ide Drive
Spokane, WA 99201

Canada

Ontario Food Terminal
165 The Queensway
Toronto, 560 Canada

Greater Montreal Central
Market
Rue Du Marche Central
Montreal, 11, Quebec

Appendix E
Sources of Useful Pamphlets and Periodicals

Write to each of these sources of diverse, valuable publications and request their most recent listing of pamphlets, leaflets and booklets. NASCO also publishes an extremely useful annotated bibliography.

Consumer Information
Public Documents
Distribution Center
Pueblo, Colorado 81009

North American Student
Cooperative Organization
(NASCO) Box 1301
Ann Arbor, Michigan 48106

United States Department
of Agriculture
c/o Superintendent of
Documents
U.S. Government Printing
Office

The Co-operative League of
the U.S.A.
1828 L Street Northwest
Washington, D.C. 20036

Washington, D.C. 20402
(Write to Home Economics
Research Division; Con-
sumer & Marketing Service;
Home and Garden Bulle-
tins.)

U.S. Department of Health,
Education and Welfare
Public Health Service
F.D.A.
5600 Fishers Lane
Rockville, Maryland 20852

Write for current sub-
scription information for
the following periodicals.

Community Nutrition Institute
Newsletter Department
2029 K Street Northwest
Washington, D.C. 20006

Co-op News
Consumers Cooperative of
Berkeley, Inc.
1414 University Avenue
Berkeley, California 94702

Food Co-op Nooz
Food Co-op Project — Loop
College
64 E. Lake Street
Chicago, Illinois 60601

Media & Consumer
Magazine
P.O. Box 111
Uxbridge, Massachusetts
01569

New Harbinger
c/o NASCO
2546 S.A.B.
Ann Arbor, Michigan 48104

The Packer
Vance Publishing Corp.
One Gateway Center
5th at State
Kansas City, Kansas 66101

Bibliography

Anderson, Glenn M., *A Better Way,* Common Bond, Inc., Minneapolis, Minn., 1972.

Anthony, Robert N., *Essentials of Accounting,* Addison-Wesley Publishing Co., Reading, Mass. Available from NASCO.

Bateson, Gregory, *Steps to an Ecology of Mind,* Ballantine Books, New York, N.Y., 1972.

Bemis, Edward W., *Co-operation in New England,* Johns Hopkins University, Baltimore, Md., 1888.

Burley, Orin E., *The Consumers' Cooperative as a Distributive Agency,* McGraw-Hill, New York, N.Y., 1939.

Coady, M.M., *Masters of Their Own Destiny,* Harper, New York, N.Y., 1939.

Cole, G.D.H., *A Century of Co-operation,* George Allen and Unwin, Ltd., London, 1944.

Curhan, Ronald C., and Edward G. Wertheim, *Consumers' Cooperatives: A Preliminary Report,* Boston University, Boston, Mass. 1973.

Dodge, Philip J., *A New Look at Cooperatives,* Public Affairs Committee, Inc., 381 Park Avenue South, New York, N.Y., 1972.

Fowler, Bertram B., *The Cooperative Challenge,* Little, Brown and Company, Boston, Mass. 1967.

Gide, Charles, *Consumers' Cooperative Societies,* The Cooperative Union, Ltd., Manchester, England, 1921.

Groves, Frank, *Cooperative Communications, Member Relations, Motivation and Behavioral Studies,* U.C.C., Madison, Wisconsin, 1933.

Harris, Emerson P., *Cooperation: The Hope of the Consumer,* The Macmillan Company, New York, N.Y., 1918.

Holyoake, George J., *The History of Cooperation in England: Its Literature and Its Advocates,* Trubner and Company, London, 1875.

Kanter, Rosabeth Moss, *Commitment and Community,* Harvard University Press, Cambridge, Mass. 1972.

Knapp, Joseph G., *The Rise of American Cooperative Enterprise: 1620–1920,* Interstate Printers and Publishers, Inc., Danville, Ill., 1969.

Kostelanetz, Richard, ed., *Beyond Left and Right,* William Morrow and Co., New York, N.Y., 1968.

Laidlaw, A.F., *Training and Extension in the Cooperative Movement,* F.A.O., Rome, 1962.

Lincoln, Murray D., *Vice President in Charge of Revolution,* McGraw-Hill, New York, N.Y., 1960.

Miller, Raymond W., *A Conservative Looks at Cooperatives,* Ohio University Press, Athens, Ohio, 1964.

Roy, Ewell Paul, *Cooperatives: Today and Tomorrow,* Interstate Printers and Publishers, Danville, Ill., 1964.

Schumacher, E.F., *Small Is Beautiful,* Harper & Row, New York, N.Y., 1973.

Sonnichsen, Albert, *Consumers' Cooperation,* The Macmillan Company, New York, N.Y., 1919.

Voorhis, Jerry, *American Cooperatives,* Harper & Bros., New York, N.Y., 1961.

United Front Press, *Food Price Blackmail,* U.F.P., Box 40099, San Francisco, Calif. 94140.

About the Author

TONY VELLELA is one of the eleven founders of New York City's largest volunteer food co-op, the Broadway Local. (The organization now numbers 400 families.) As a consultant, he helps groups to start and build food co-ops.

Mr. Vellela is a new culture journalist covering consumer affairs. His work has appeared in the *Christian Science Monitor, Crawdaddy, Moneysworth, Rodale Press, Rolling Stone,* the N.E.A. and Bell-McClure newspaper syndicates. He lives on the Upper West Side of Manhattan.